Grades 1–2

Successful Strategies
for Reading in the
Content Areas

2nd Edition

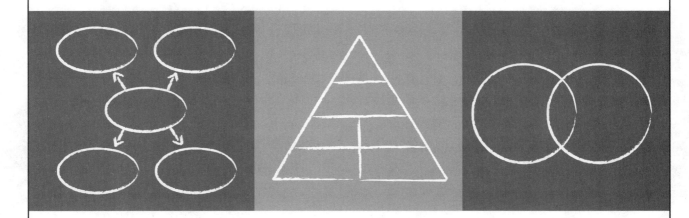

SHELL EDUCATION

Successful Strategies
for Reading in the Content Areas
2nd Edition

Grades 1–2

Editor
Conni Medina

Assistant Editor
Leslie Huber, M.A.

Senior Editor
Lori Kamola, M.S.Ed.

Editor-in-Chief
Sharon Coan, M.S.Ed.

Editorial Manager
Gisela Lee, M.A.

Creative Director
Lee Aucoin

Cover Design
Neri Garcia

Imaging
Sandra Riley
Don Tran

Authors
TCM Staff

Publisher
Corinne Burton, M.A.Ed.

Shell Education
5301 Oceanus Drive
Huntington Beach, CA 92649
1-877-777-3450
http://www.shelleducation.com
ISBN 978-1-4258-0468-8
©2008 Shell Education
Made in U.S.A.

Table of Contents

Introduction

The saying "Every teacher is a teacher of reading" is well known but not always true. It is usually regarded as the task of the English or language arts teacher to guide students through the effective use of comprehension strategies as they read. Although students read in almost every subject area they study, content-area teachers typically overlook the need for guiding students through their textbook-based and trade book-based reading tasks. Comprehension strategies best serve students when they are employed across the curricula and in the context of their actual learning. It is only then that students can independently use the strategies successfully when reading. Students typically read literature or fictional stories for English or language arts, but they will spend the majority of their adulthood reading nonfiction, expository writing. The strategies that students use to comprehend literature are different from those they use for nonfiction. It is important to note that around grades four and five, educators see a drop in reading achievement. At this time, students seem to lose interest in reading independently, spend less time reading for pleasure, and struggle more to read the materials required of them at school. It is for this reason that all teachers at all levels must actively pursue ways to greatly enhance their students' abilities to understand reading material, and this can be accomplished by working directly with reading comprehension strategies.

How to Use This Book

Reading comprehension is a complex process involving interactions between the reader and the text, using multiple skills. Students need a variety of strategies to be successful readers. *Successful Strategies for Reading in the Content Areas,* 2nd Edition contains a variety of reading strategies that will help increase comprehension. This updated edition has grouped the strategies and skills to match the seven categories of strategies and skills taught in *Exploring Nonfiction: A Differentiated Content-Area Reading Program* (Teacher Created Materials Publishing 2008). An additional section, titled Developing Vocabulary, is also provided in this book. This book is divided into the following sections:

- **Monitor Comprehension** (including **Set the Purpose** and **Author's Point of View**)
- **Activate and Connect**
- **Infer Meaning**
- **Ask Questions**
- **Determine Importance** (including **Main Idea and Supporting Details, Text Structures, Text Organizers,** and **Using Parts of the Book**)
- **Visualize**
- **Summarize and Synthesize**
- **Developing Vocabulary**

Introduction

How to Use This Book *(cont.)*

Each of these eight sections contains an introduction, teaching strategies, and reproducible templates for students. Many of the teaching strategies have corresponding graphic organizers or other templates included, with page number references to direct you to the correct reproducible page. It is important to read the introduction to each section before using the strategies in order to understand how best to teach these important nonfiction skills. For further information, and to understand the research about reading comprehension and content-area reading, read the rest of this introduction. You will also find a Correlation to Standards chart (pages 14–16) showing the national standards to which each strategy is aligned. A CD is provided at the back of this book with all of the graphic organizers and templates in PDF format so you can print them. Most of these pages are also provided in Microsoft Word so that they can be modified. An index of these pages is provided on the CD.

This book provides a wealth of information about content-area reading strategies and skills that can be used with any nonfiction text. The strategies and skills can also be used in conjunction with *Exploring Nonfiction: A Differentiated Content-Area Reading Program* as a resource guide to support the lesson plans. Refer to the Works Cited (pages 275–76) for a list of references used to create this book.

Research: Explicit Instruction of Reading Comprehension Strategies

If content-area teachers were asked how they improve their students' reading skills, the majority would most likely struggle to answer the question. Good teachers use many strategies to enhance students' reading comprehension, and it is helpful to identify which strategies they use in order to explain why the techniques successfully improve their students' skills. Even more important is the explicit instruction of the individual strategies, including modeling, guided practice, and independent practice. These steps ensure that students learn to independently and consistently use a wide variety of reading comprehension strategies for a broad range of reading experiences.

Teaching students the strategies to improve their comprehension is nothing new to educators. Extensive research has demonstrated that students greatly benefit from the direct instruction of reading comprehension strategies when reading a text (Duke and Pearson 2002; Block 1999; Dole, Brown, and Trathen 1996; Durkin 1978; Pressley and Afflerbach 1995, as cited by Kragler, Walker, and Martin 2005). Simply put, strategy instruction is an effective means of assisting students in improving comprehension and understanding. This book, *Successful Strategies for Reading in the Content Areas*, 2nd Edition, is designed to give content-area teachers tools for teaching reading comprehension strategies.

Introduction

Research: Which Strategies to Teach

The National Reading Panel Report (2000), commissioned by the U.S. Congress to evaluate research in the area of reading, identified a number of effective comprehension strategies. Pressley (2000) echoes these findings. These strategies include vocabulary development, prediction skills (including inference), the building of prior knowledge, think-alouds, visual representations, summarization, and questioning. This book provides an explanation of these strategies and describes a number of activities that content-area teachers can incorporate into their lessons. These findings guide the selection of strategies included in *Successful Strategies for Reading in the Content Areas.*

Students also need to develop their metacognitive skills when reading and learning. Scholars agree that metacognition plays a significant role in reading comprehension (Baker and Brown 1984; Garner 1987; Mastropieri and Scruggs 1997; Paris, Wasik, and Turner 1991; Schraw 1998, as cited by Baker 2002). Research shows that teachers should foster metacognition and comprehension monitoring during comprehension instruction because students will be able to better monitor and self-regulate their abilities to read. "Developing engaged readers involves helping students to become both strategic and aware of the strategies they use to read" (McCarthy, Hoffman, and Galda 1999, as cited by Baker 2002).

It is important to note that teachers should never take a "one size fits all" approach when teaching reading comprehension. Some strategies work for some students, and other strategies work for other students, just as some strategies work best with certain types of reading material, and other strategies work best with other types of reading material. The most important thing to remember when trying to improve reading comprehension in students is that the skill level, group dynamic, and makeup of the students should determine the approach to take.

Research: The Steps Involved in Explicit Instruction of Reading Comprehension Strategies

According to Duke and Pearson (2002), research supports that a balanced approach to teaching reading comprehension is more than teaching students specific reading strategies and providing opportunities to read. Teachers should begin with direct explanation and instruction of how to use the strategies so that after a series of steps, students will be able to use the strategies independently. The following are the five steps for explicit instruction of comprehension strategies:

1. **Provide an exact description of the strategy and explain when and how it should be used.** Teachers need to explain what the strategy is called, why students should use it, what it helps them understand, and how often they should use it.

2. **Provide modeling of the strategy.** Teachers should model how to use the strategy when students are in the process of reading. Students can also model the strategy while the teacher reinforces an explanation of how the strategy is being used.

3. **Provide opportunities for collaborative use of the strategy in action.** Teachers and students should work together and share their use of the strategy while they are reading.

4. **Lead guided practice sessions using the strategy, and allow for a gradual release of responsibility from the teacher to the student.** At this stage, teachers can remind students of how to use the strategy and of the steps involved, but teachers should allow students to work on the technique independently.

5. **Encourage students' independent use of the strategy.** In the final stage, teachers might gently remind students of the name of the strategy, but the students should be using the technique automatically and independently.

Duke and Pearson (2002) emphasize the importance of remembering that students need to be able to use more than one comprehension strategy to understand a reading selection. Throughout the five phases, other strategies should be referenced and modeled for the students. When working with reading materials in any content area, teachers should use the very same techniques to introduce a new learning strategy to students as they would during language arts or in an English class. Research shows that students can master the use of reading comprehension strategies when instruction follows the five steps listed above. When covering any topic, teachers must take the time to allow students to master the strategy so that they can become independent readers. Follow these steps with the strategies in this book, and students will improve their comprehension.

Introduction

Research: What Great Teachers Do

Many content-area teachers use a variety of strategies that go beyond simply answering the questions at the end of the chapter. Research shows, however, that there is a big difference between teaching reading comprehension strategies well and teaching them in a dynamic, ingenious way that motivates and excites students about reading and learning. Through research, observations, and conversations with teachers who have been successful with the direct instruction of reading comprehension strategies, Keene (2002) has identified five traits specific to outstanding and consistently effective teachers. What makes these teachers effective?

1. **They take the time to understand each strategy in their own reading.** Reading about the techniques and activities is not enough. Great teachers of reading comprehension strategies take the time to figure out how to use and understand every strategy with the texts they are reading. In doing so, they increase their own metacognitive skills and can better articulate their own thinking during reading.

2. **They incorporate reading comprehension strategy instruction into predictable daily, weekly, and monthly activities.** Effective teachers of reading comprehension strategies set goals for strategy learning and create a predictable schedule to ensure that those goals are met. These teachers also set aside time to work more intensively with small groups as needed. They also set aside time for students to reflect on their progress toward the goals they set.

3. **They ask students to apply each comprehension strategy to a wide variety of texts and text levels in different contexts.** Great teachers use beautifully written texts with challenging and profound themes that can be read in their entirety in a mini-lesson. For example, they ask students to summarize a textbook and a short story, use sensory images in poetry and expository essays, and use background knowledge to understand a biography and letters to the editor. In order to comprehend actively and assertively, students must read texts with appropriately challenging words and concepts.

4. **They vary the size of groupings for strategy instruction.** Changing the group size and configuration helps teachers focus on different goals during comprehension-strategy instruction.

    Large groups are best for:

    - introducing a new strategy
    - modeling think-alouds to show students how good readers use the strategy
    - practicing think-alouds with new genres, and allowing students to share their experiences using the strategy

Introduction

Research: What Great Teachers Do *(cont.)*

Small groups are best for:

- providing more intensive instruction for students who need it
- introducing gifted students to the strategy so that they can apply it independently to more challenging texts and new genres
- introducing new activities that enable students to share their thinking (maps, charts, thinking notebooks, sketches, logs, etc.)
- allowing students to discuss books and comprehension strategies without teacher involvement

Conferences are best for:

- checking a student's understanding of how to apply the strategies he or she is studying to his or her own books
- providing intensive strategy instruction for texts that may be particularly challenging to a student
- coaching a student in how he or she might reveal his or her thinking to others
- pushing a student to use strategies to think more deeply than he or she might have imagined possible

5. **They gradually release the responsibility for the application of a comprehension strategy to the students.** Great teachers follow the steps involved in the explicit instruction of reading comprehension strategies (Duke and Pearson 2002): over several weeks, teachers provide thorough explanations of the strategy, model how to use it, allow for group work with the strategy, transition to more independent use, and then release the responsibility to the students.

By following these guidelines for the teacher and using the strategies in this book, students will be provided with rich and meaningful opportunities for comprehension instruction.

Introduction

Research: What Do Good Readers Do When They Read?

Duke and Pearson (2002) have established that good readers:

- read actively

- set goals for their reading tasks and constantly evaluate whether the text and their reading of it is meeting their goals

- preview the text prior to reading, noting the text organization and structure in order to locate the sections most relevant to their reading goals

- make predictions about what is to come in the text

- read selectively, continually making decisions about their reading process: what to read carefully, what to read quickly, what to skim, what not to read, and what to reread

- construct, revise, and question the meanings they develop as they read

- determine the meanings of unfamiliar or unknown words and concepts in the text

- draw from, compare, and integrate their prior knowledge with the material in the text

- consider the authors of the text, their styles, beliefs, intentions, historical perspectives, and so on

- monitor their understanding of the text, make adjustments in their reading as necessary, and deal with inconsistencies or gaps as needed

- evaluate the text's quality and value, and interact with the text both intellectually and emotionally

- read different kinds of texts differently

- construct and revise summaries of what they have read when reading expository texts

- think about the text before, during, and after reading

- feel satisfied and productive when reading, even though comprehension is a consuming, continuous, and complex activity

Content-area teachers can easily incorporate the same techniques that language arts teachers have used for years to help students become more strategic and skilled readers and to help them comprehend the materials they encounter. Teachers will find the job of using the textbook much easier if every student has the skills of a good reader.

Opportunities for all of the activities above are provided in the strategies listed throughout this book.

Research: The Reading Process

Teachers need to understand the steps of the reading process in order to help students improve their reading comprehension skills. Content-area teachers can easily optimize the use of reading materials with students by utilizing the three-part framework of the reading process to facilitate learning. Break reading assignments into three comprehension-building steps: before reading, during reading, and after reading (Pressley 2002). It is important to note that what teachers do during each stage of the reading process is crucial to their students' learning.

Before Reading

Prior to beginning a reading assignment, engage in a variety of activities in the hopes of reducing any uncertainty involved in the reading task. These activities include generating interest in the topic, building and activating prior knowledge, and setting a purpose for reading.

Teachers who motivate students and create interest prior to assigning the reading improve their students' overall comprehension. Students who are more motivated to read are more engaged and actively involved in the process of learning than those who are not motivated. Motivated readers are also more likely to have better long-term recall of what they read.

Teachers can motivate students by assessing their prior knowledge. Knowing students' background knowledge on a topic makes it easier to build on and activate that knowledge during reading. The mind holds information in the form of frameworks called *schemata*, and as we learn new information, we store it in a framework of what we already know. Teachers who build on and activate students' prior knowledge before reading prepare students to more efficiently comprehend the material that they will be reading.

Prior to reading, teachers should prepare students to read by setting a purpose for the reading task. There are a number of different purposes a student can have for a reading assignment: predict what will happen, learn new vocabulary, summarize the information, evaluate the author's point of view, and so on. Students need to know what their purpose is as they read because it helps them focus their efforts. In doing so, teachers can guide the students' search for meaning as they read.

Teachers should also take the time to introduce key concepts and vocabulary prior to reading. In doing so, they help students read the selection more fluently, with greater automaticity, and with greater comprehension—all of which lead to greater recall of the information.

Finally, teachers should establish in their students a metacognitive awareness for the task of reading. Students should be prompted to be aware of what they are thinking and doing as they are reading. Developing metacognitive awareness allows students to better understand the strategies necessary for effective learning. It also enables students to take control of their own learning, making them more independent readers and learners.

Introduction

Research: The Reading Process *(cont.)*

During Reading

During reading, students are actively reading text aloud or silently. During this stage of the reading process, students are engaged in answering questions (either self-generated or teacher-generated), monitoring their comprehension of the text, clarifying the purpose of reading, visualizing the information, and building connections.

Most often, students are engaged in answering questions while they read. Proficient readers self-question as they read to make sure they understand the reading material. In addition, students search for the answers to questions they may have generated prior to reading. As students process the text, they begin to infer what the author intended, and they begin to generalize about the specific details in the information provided. They also look for support for the predictions they have made.

Students are involved in monitoring and regulating their reading abilities while they are actively reading. If a section of the text is confusing, students need to know that they can reread the section, use fix-up strategies to help them understand what they are puzzled by, or adjust the speed of their reading to suit their purposes and the difficulty of the text. Thus, students must monitor their own reading strategies and make modifications as needed.

In addition to monitoring their reading abilities, students are also figuring out words as they actively read. If they do not know what a word means, they use the context clues or word parts to decode the meaning of the word. As students attend to vocabulary needs, they also observe the text structure and features as they read, which helps them organize the new information.

During reading, teachers can focus students' attention on the objectives of the reading task. Students may adjust their purposes for reading based on the information they are reading and on their prior knowledge.

Proficient readers actively work to create images in their minds that represent the concepts in the reading material. Teachers should engage students in creating mental images to help them comprehend the material as they are reading. This promotes greater recall of the information and engages students in the reading process.

While students are reading, they are in the process of connecting the new information they are learning to their existing schemata. Therefore, teachers should be actively involved in helping students make connections between what they already know and what they are learning. This prepares them for the synthesis of the information. Teachers can be instrumental in helping students relate to the material.

Introduction

Research: The Reading Process *(cont.)*

After Reading

Students expand their understanding of the material after reading the text. During the final stage of the reading process, students build connections among the bits of information that they have read, enabling them to deepen their understanding and reflect on what they have learned.

After reading, students need the teacher to guide them through follow-up exercises so they can reflect on what they have read. During reflection, students can contemplate the new information, clarify new ideas, refine their thinking, and connect what they have learned to other ideas in order to synthesize the new information. Teachers should spend time revisiting the text with students to demonstrate that the reading experience is not a single event.

Also, students generally find the main idea and distinguish the most important ideas from less important ideas. This enables them to prioritize and summarize what they have read.

After reading, teachers generally assess what students have learned. Students answer questions about what they have learned, and teachers generally use their answers to determine whether the students can move on or need additional instruction. Teachers can take advantage of additional activities for after reading to deepen students' comprehension of the text.

After students have read, they are able to engage in higher-level thinking tasks. Students can use critical thinking to evaluate the quality or validity of the material, or they can synthesize what they have learned by integrating their new knowledge with their prior knowledge. They can also analyze what they have read by closely examining the text characteristics specific to the genre.

Introduction

Correlation to Standards

The No Child Left Behind (NCLB) legislation mandates that all states adopt academic standards that identify the skills students will learn in kindergarten through grade 12. While many states had already adopted academic standards prior to NCLB, the legislation set requirements to ensure that the standards were detailed and comprehensive.

Standards are designed to focus instruction and guide adoption of curricula. Standards are statements that describe the criteria necessary for students to meet specific academic goals. They define the knowledge, skills, and content students should acquire at each level. Standards are also used to develop standardized tests to evaluate students' academic progress.

In many states today, teachers are required to demonstrate how their lessons meet state standards. State standards are used in the development of Shell Education products, so educators can be assured that they meet the academic requirements of each state.

How to Find Your State Correlations

Shell Education is committed to producing educational materials that are research- and standards-based. In this effort, all products are correlated to the academic standards of the 50 states, the District of Columbia, and the Department of Defense Dependent Schools. A correlation report customized for your state can be printed directly from the following website: **http://www.shelleducation.com**. If you require assistance in printing correlation reports, please contact customer service at 1-877-777-3450.

McREL Compendium

Shell Education uses the Mid-continent Research for Education and Learning (McREL) Compendium to create standards correlations. Each year, McREL analyzes state standards and revises the compendium. By following this procedure, McREL is able to produce a general compilation of national standards.

Each reading comprehension strategy assessed in this book is based on one or more McREL content standards. The chart on pages 15–16 shows the McREL standards that correlate to each strategy provided in the book.

Introduction

Correlation to Standards *(cont.)*

Standard/Objective	Page (Strategy)
5.1—Uses mental images based on pictures to aid in comprehension of text	41(10); 42(14, 16); 43(17); 69(11); 88(8); 89(9); 90(14); 131(2); 133(5); 134(6, 7); 135(8, 9, 10); 136(12, 13, 14); 154(3, 4); 155(5); 156(8, 9, 10); 157(11, 12); 158(13, 14, 16, 17); 175(1); 176(5); 178(10); 179(15, 16); 197(5); 198(10); 213(1, 2, 3); 214(4, 5, 6); 215(7, 8, 9, 10); 216(11, 12, 13, 14); 217(15); 218(16, 17, 18); 219(19, 20); 220(21, 22); 235(1); 236(3, 4); 237(6, 7); 238(8, 9); 259(1, 2, 3); 260(5, 7); 262(13, 14); 263(16)
5.2—Uses meaning clues (e.g., picture captions, titles, covers, headings, story structures, story topics) to aid in comprehension and make predictions about content (e.g., actions, events, character's behavior)	24(7,8); 25(9, 10, 11); 39(3, 4); 40(6, 7, 8); 41(10, 11); 42(14, 15, 16); 43(17); 65(1, 2, 3); 66(5); 67(6, 7); 68(10); 69(11); 70(12); 71(14); 87(2); 87(5, 8); 89(9, 10, 11, 12); 90(13, 14); 111(1); 112(3); 113(4); 115(8); 131(1, 2); 132(3); 134(7); 135(9, 11); 136(12, 13, 14); 154(1, 4); 155(5); 157(11, 12); 158(14, 15, 16, 17); 175(1); 176(3, 4, 5); 177(6, 7, 8, 9); 178(10, 11, 12, 13); 179(14, 15, 16); 197(1, 2, 3, 4, 5); 198(6, 7, 8, 9, 10); 213(1); 216(11, 12, 13, 14); 218(17, 18); 219(20); 220(21); 235(1); 236(2, 3, 4); 237(6, 7); 238(8, 9); 239(10); 240(13); 259(1); 260(7); 261(10, 11); 262(12, 15); 263(16)
5.4—Uses basic elements of structural analysis (e.g., syllables, basic prefixes, suffixes, root words, compound words, spelling patterns, contractions) to decode unknown words	135(9); 154(1); 175(2); 176(5); 198(9, 10); 259(1, 2, 3); 260(4, 5, 6, 7); 261(8, 10, 11); 262(12, 13, 15); 263(16, 17)
5.6—Understands level-appropriate sight words and vocabulary (e.g., words for persons, places, things, actions; high-frequency words such as said, was, and where)	38(1); 39(2, 3, 4); 40(7); 67(6); 112(3); 154(1, 4); 155(6); 158(17); 175(2); 176(5); 179(15); 198(7, 9, 10); 218(17); 259(1, 2, 3); 260(4, 5, 6, 7); 261(8, 9, 10, 11); 262(13, 14, 15); 263(16, 17)
5.7—Uses self-correction strategies (e.g., searches for cues, identifies miscues, rereads, asks for help)	70(12); 89(11); 113(4); 154(1); 177(6); 198(9); 259(1, 2, 3); 260(6); 261(11); 262(13, 15); 263(16, 17)
7.1—Uses reading skills and strategies to understand a variety of informational texts (e.g., written directions, signs, captions, warning labels, informational books)	25(10, 11); 38(1); 39(3, 4); 40(7, 8, 9); 43(18); 68(10); 69(11); 71(14); 88(6); 112(3); 117(10); 131(1, 2); 133(5); 134(6, 7); 135(8, 9, 11); 136(12, 14); 154(1, 3); 155(5, 6, 7); 156(8, 9, 10); 157(11, 12); 158(13, 14, 15, 16, 17); 175(1, 2); 176(3, 4, 5); 177(7, 8, 9); 178(10, 11, 12, 13); 179(14, 15, 16); 197(2, 3, 4, 5); 198(6, 7, 9, 10); 213(1, 2); 215(7); 218(16, 18); 219(20); 220(23); 236(2); 237(6, 7); 238(8, 9); 239(10); 240(13); 260(7); 262(14)

Introduction

Correlation to Standards *(cont.)*

Standard/Objective	Page (Strategy)
7.2—Understands the main idea and supporting details of simple expository information	41(11); 42(16); 43(18, 19, 20); 70(12); 88(6); 112(3); 113(4); 131(1, 2); 132(3); 134(6, 7); 135(8, 9, 10, 11); 136(12, 14); 154(3, 4); 155(5, 6, 7); 156(8, 9, 10); 157(11, 12); 158(13, 14, 15, 16, 17); 176(5); 177(6, 7, 8, 9); 178(11, 12); 179(15, 16); 197(4); 213(1, 2); 215(9); 217(5); 218(16, 18); 220(23); 235(1); 236(2, 3, 4); 237(5, 6, 7); 238(8, 9); 239(10, 11); 240(12, 13, 14, 15, 16); 260(7)
7.3—Summarizes information found in texts (e.g., retells in own words)	41(11); 42(14); 90(13); 115(8); 134(7); 154(3, 4); 156(8, 9); 157(11, 12); 158(14); 177(6, 9); 178(12); 179(14, 15); 198(6); 217(5); 218(16, 18); 235(1); 236(2, 3, 4); 237(5, 6, 7); 238(8, 9); 239(10, 11); 240(12, 13, 14, 15, 16)
7.4—Relates new information to prior knowledge and experience	22(1, 2); 23(3, 4, 5); 25(10, 11); 39(2, 3); 40(5, 6); 41(10, 13); 42(14, 15, 16); 43(17); 65(1, 2); 66(4, 5); 67(7, 8); 68(9); 70(12); 71(13, 14); 87(1, 2, 4); 88(5); 89(9); 112(2); 115(8); 117(1); 132(4); 133(5); 134(6, 7); 135(10); 136(13); 154(3); 155(6); 156(8, 9, 10); 157(11, 12); 158(13, 14); 176(3); 177(8); 198(6); 213(1, 3); 214(4, 5, 6); 215(8, 10); 217(5); 218(16); 219(20); 220(21, 22, 23); 235(1); 236(2); 238(8, 9); 240(12); 260(7); 261(8); 262(14); 263(16, 17)
8.2—Asks and responds to questions (e.g., about the meaning of a story, about the meaning of words or ideas)	23(4, 6); 40(6, 8); 41(13); 42(14); 65(1, 3); 66(4, 5); 68(9); 68(10); 71(14); 87(2); 88(5, 6, 7, 8); 89(9, 10, 11, 12); 90(13); 111(1); 112(2); 113(4, 5); 114(6, 7); 115(8, 9); 117(10, 11); 132(3, 4); 133(5); 135(9, 10); 136(12); 155(7); 157(11); 158(13, 16); 175(1); 176(4); 197(1, 2, 4); 219(19); 220(23); 237(5); 238(9); 239(10); 240(14)
8.5—Uses level-appropriate vocabulary in speech (e.g., number words; words that describe people, places, things, events, locations, actions; synonyms, antonyms; homonyms, word analogies, common figures of speech)	40(8, 9); 41(12, 13); 42(15); 43(18); 65(1, 3); 67(6); 68(9); 87(3, 4); 90(13, 14); 117(11); 132(4); 154(2); 155(7); 158(16, 17); 175(1); 177(7, 8, 9); 178(12); 179(14, 16); 197(4, 5); 214(4, 5, 6); 215(8, 9); 217(5); 218(17); 237(5); 239(10, 11); 240(13, 15); 260(5); 261(10, 11); 262(12, 13, 14, 15); 263(17)

Monitor Comprehension

PASSPORT TO COMPREHENSION

#50468 Successful Strategies

Monitor Comprehension—Set the Purpose

Nonfiction texts can be used to spark students' interests in a topic and encourage them to want to read on to learn more about the topic. Quite often, though, students begin reading a text without knowing why they are reading it and without knowing the expected outcomes. Students who can clearly identify and state the purpose for reading will be more likely to make meaningful and relevant responses in answering questions that relate to the text. By having a sense of purpose or a final goal in mind, students are able to focus attention on the important facts and details and pay less attention to the minor facts and irrelevant details.

Establishing or setting a purpose for reading makes a significant difference in students' concentration and abilities to recall the information at a later time. The teacher needs to guide students into setting a purpose for reading the text by:

- having students make predictions about the text by looking at the cover (title, author, pictures)
- asking "What do you think will happen in the text?"
- developing a list of questions that students would like to have answered

By doing these things, the teacher is focusing students' attention on thinking and learning about the topic. This focus will enhance students' abilities to read, comprehend, and remember the information that has just been read.

The Purpose for Reading Nonfiction Texts

Nonfiction texts are read for many reasons (Cunningham and Allington 1999). Some of the reasons are to:

- answer questions
- ask questions
- encourage the use of critical thinking skills
- stimulate students' interests and curiosity
- create a sense of wonder
- develop a greater understanding of people, places, and things
- increase students' vocabulary
- help students connect the information in the text to their own personal experiences and the real world
- increase students' background knowledge on a topic
- examine the graphic elements (pictures, charts, graphs, etc.) to gain additional information

By setting a purpose for reading, students have a structure for learning that makes it easier to identify the key points and important facts and details.

Monitor Comprehension— Set the Purpose

Text Selection

When choosing books for a certain purpose, the teacher needs to keep in mind five different factors:

1. The readability of the text: is the text appropriate for the age, interest, and reading level of each student?

2. The subject or topic of the text or reading selection: is the reading selection appropriate for the age, interest, and reading level of each student?

3. The author: books by certain authors automatically gain the students' undivided attention.

4. The content: How is the subject matter presented in the text? Are there any eye-catching graphic features (pictures, illustrations, charts, etc.) used in the text? How many words are there on a page? How much of the text can students read independently?

5. Reason for reading: is the text being read to build students' background information, to have the students practice a specific reading strategy, or to answer specific questions on the topic?

The Purpose for Selecting a Text

When selecting a text, the teacher needs to model the thought processes involved in selecting the text. Some of the questions the teachers (or students) need to ask themselves are:

- What information can I learn from this text?
- What reading strategies can I model and practice using this text?
- How will the text build my background knowledge?
- How can the text be used in classroom discussions?

The Teacher's Choices

A teacher can use nonfiction texts to teach a wide variety of subjects. When a teacher selects a text for students to read, the text should (Harvey and Goudvis 2000):

- be well written
- spark the students' imaginations
- allow for different interpretations
- make students think
- be logically organized
- be easy for students to understand
- use clear and vivid language
- be appropriate for the age and interest of each student

Monitor Comprehension— Set the Purpose

Choosing Appropriate Materials to Read

Students are more likely to become interested and motivated to read a text if it is written at their current reading level. By selecting an independent reading text that is at the appropriate level, students will be able to practice different reading strategies successfully, become more fluent readers, and develop a lifelong love of reading.

Readability

Readability plays a role in whether or not students will be able to successfully read and understand the nonfiction text. Many aspects need to be taken into consideration when deciding if the readability of a text is appropriate for the students.

- Is the text of interest to the students? If students have an interest in the topic, then they will become motivated to read the text.
- Is the text well written? Will it grab students' attention? This will make students want to read the text.
- Are there too many new ideas and/or too much new information being presented in the text? This can be extremely frustrating for students because they are trying to read, learn, and recall the information all at the same time.
- How legible is the print? If the print is too small or if there are many words on one page, these features can inhibit students' desire to read the text.
- What kinds of words and sentence structures are used in the text? How do they relate to the students? Students with strong reading skills will not be interested in reading a simple text. By the same token, students with weak reading skills will be frustrated trying to decode a text with many multisyllabic words and complex sentence structures.

Strategies Students Can Use in Selecting a Book

Research shows that texts that can grab students' interests are texts that encourage students not only to read more but also to improve their reading fluency and comprehension skills. When selecting books for independent reading, students need to select books that:

- interest them
- serve a certain purpose—reading for information, for an answer to a question, for personal enjoyment, etc.
- are at their reading level

The strategies on the following pages will help guide students to set their own purposes for reading nonfiction texts.

Monitor Comprehension— Set the Purpose

Strategy 1: List, Group, and Label

List, Group, and Label is a prereading strategy that builds background knowledge, uses the students' own knowledge on the topic as a foundation for learning new information, and provides a structure for students to organize information (Rasinski and Padak 2000). When using List, Group, and Label, students brainstorm as many words as possible that relate to the topic being studied. Once the list is made, students sort the words into categories based on common characteristics. (Standard 7.4)

After all of the words have been sorted, students label each set of words and can add new words to the different lists. An activity to use with this strategy is on page 26. The following example is a guide.

Topic: Dogs

Brainstorm List			Label: Kinds of Dogs	Label: Parts of a Dog	Label: Dog Stuff
wet nose	playful	paws	Dalmatian	wet nose	dog house
veterinarian	bowl	Poodle	Chihuahua	dog breath	food
dog house	stinky	bowl	hunting	ears	bones
Dalmatian	hunting	smelly	Terrier	paws	treats
protection	whine	bath	Poodle	tail	brush
Chihuahua	treats	collar			water
dog breath	brush	leash			bowl
food	ears	tail			collar
bones	Terrier	tricks			leash
fleas	fun	bark			
furry	water				

Strategy 2: Word Sort

Word sorts can be used as a prereading strategy that prepares students for the information that will be covered in the text. Word sorts allow students to:

- share what they already know on the topic
- provide a purpose for reading the text
- increase their curiosity on the topic

Word sorts are very similar to the List, Group, and Label activity. The only difference is that when doing a word sort, the teacher provides students with a list of up to 20 words that have been taken from the text. Students organize the words into different groups and then label each group of words (Rasinski and Padak 2000). After the list has been completed, the teacher can lead students in a discussion about the topic. Students can share their expectations and predictions in regard to the text (Rasinski and Padak 2000). The template on page 27 can be used for this strategy. (Standard 7.4)

Strategy 3: Brainstorming

Brainstorming is similar to the-word sort activity and allows students to set a purpose for reading. The difference between brainstorming and a word-sort activity is that in brainstorming, students generate a list of words, while in a word-sort activity, the teacher provides students with a list of words. Students then organize the words into different groups and write a label (or title) for each group of words. A brainstorming template is provided on page 28. (Standard 7.4)

Strategy 4: KWL Chart

A teacher can support students' abilities to set a purpose for reading by having them develop predictions and ask questions about the topic before reading the text. This can be achieved with a KWL chart. The KWL chart organizes information into three categories: "What Do I Know," "What Do I Want to Learn," and "What Did I Learn." See the template on page 29. (Standards 7.4, 8.2)

Strategy 5: Anticipation Guides

Anticipation guides can be used to activate students' prior knowledge on a topic, set a purpose for reading/learning, and kindle students' interests in the topic. Before reading the text, the teacher writes several statements about the topic on a piece of paper or on a transparency. The statements contain ideas and concepts that students should think about and discuss before reading the text. After reading the text, the teacher returns students' attention to the anticipation guide and discusses each statement. Students can reaffirm each statement with supporting evidence from the text or change their point of view based upon the newly learned information (Rasinksi and Padak 2000). The templates on pages 30 and 31 work with this strategy. (Standard 7.4)

Strategy 6: "I Wonder" Statements

"I Wonder" statements can be used to set a purpose for further learning. "I Wonder" statements are a natural, authentic outcome of students' natural curiosities about everything and everyone around them. They are the "burning questions" that students have about a topic, and those "burning questions" make students want to research the topic to find answers. A teacher can encourage students to wonder about the topic through the use of authentic questioning and by helping students find answers to their questions. The teacher should model using "I Wonder" statements often in the classroom. When reading from a nonfiction text, the teacher stops at appropriate moments and says, "I wonder . . . (filling in as appropriate)." This will show students that it is important to think about what they are reading and why they are reading it.

Examples of some "I Wonder" statements:

- "I wonder what baby octopuses look like. Do they have eight arms when they are born?"
- "I wonder what kinds of fish are enemies of the octopus. I think sharks might try to eat an octopus, but I'm not sure."

The template on page 32 can be used for this strategy. (Standard 8.2)

Monitor Comprehension— Set the Purpose

Strategy 7: Surveying the Text

The act of surveying is an important prereading strategy to use when reading nonfiction text because it allows students to have some measure of control over the text. Through the act of surveying, students are able to set a purpose for learning. Surveying will also stimulate students' interest in the topic and will make it easier for students to understand and recall the important facts and details presented in the text. In surveying the text, the teacher has students examine the different parts of the book to obtain an overview of how the text is organized. Provide ample time for students to browse through their textbooks and become familiar and comfortable with them. The teacher should model how to survey the text so that students will understand how this is a helpful skill. Understanding how the text is organized will make it easier for them to identify the key points that will be presented in the text and learn in advance the author's message. Use the template on page 33 with this strategy. (Standard 5.2)

When surveying the text, students will examine five sections:

- table of contents
- preface
- appendix
- graphic features (charts, maps, diagrams, etc.)
- headings

The teacher can ask questions that pertain to the features outlined above. The following are some questions a teacher might ask students:

- "On what page would we be more likely to find information on the foods an octopus eats?"
- "Where should we look to find out how much an octopus grows in a year?"

Once students have surveyed the major parts of the nonfiction text, the teacher then directs students' attention to certain text clues that signal important information is being presented. These text clues include the following:

- words written in bold print
- words written in italics
- words written in different colors
- any captions under the illustrations, photographs, charts, and diagrams

Strategy 8: Taking a Picture Walk

A "picture walk" can be used to establish a purpose for reading the text. A picture walk serves as a tool that focuses students' attention on gaining information from the graphic features used in the text. When doing a picture walk, the teacher covers the text with a piece of paper or with several sticky notes. By covering the text, the teacher is demonstrating to students that information can be obtained by closely examining the pictures. The teacher's role in doing a picture walk is to encourage and guide students in a discussion about the pictures used in the text. While discussing the text, the teacher makes sure to use as much of the text's vocabulary as possible. (Standard 5.2)

Monitor Comprehension— Set the Purpose

Strategy 9: Making Predictions

Students with good reading skills make predictions before and during the reading of the text. Throughout the reading, students are able to confirm, reject, or revise predictions to reflect the learning of new information. To support these predictions, students must locate the supporting evidence and details in the text. Before reading the text, the teacher can call on individual students to share their predictions with the class. These predictions can be recorded on a piece of chart paper or on the board. The teacher should model how to make predictions with the whole class. After the teacher has done this several times, he or she can invite students to share their predictions. Then students can practice this strategy in small groups or with partners. After reading several pages or a chapter, the teacher can return students' attention to the predictions. After reading each prediction, students may decide that the prediction is correct, needs to be adjusted, or needs to be completely thrown out. Before returning to the text, the teacher can ask students to share new predictions based on what they have just read. Again, after reading several more pages or a chapter, students can re-examine their predictions. These two steps, making and confirming (or adjusting or rejecting) predictions, can be repeated throughout the process of reading. Use page 34 for practice with this strategy. (Standard 5.2)

Strategy 10: Guided Reading

Because no single strategy works for everyone, an integrated approach works best when teaching students to comprehend nonfiction text. To start, the teacher should present students with the objective or outcome that is expected from reading the nonfiction text. At this point, the teacher should also explain any vocabulary that is unfamiliar to students. Next, hold a planned discussion about the topic. This discussion should include information to activate background knowledge. Students should survey the text and predict what it is going to tell. After surveying the text, students and teacher should set purposes for reading. Predicting or using other strategies described in this section can assist the teacher in setting a purpose. The teacher should next guide students through the reading. The study guide on page 35 can aid in this task. After reading the selection, the teacher should plan activities that allow students to use the information they have gathered. After reading, the teacher can use the activity on page 36 to encourage students to think about their reading strategies. (Standards 5.2, 7.1, 7.4)

Strategy 11: Prereading Prediction

The teacher selects a nonfiction book and has students read the title of the book and look at the illustrations on the cover. Students can use the template on page 37 to write their predictions about the text. Before reading the text, the teacher can call on students to share their predictions about the text. These predictions can be recorded on a piece of chart paper or on the board. After reading several pages of the text, the teacher can return students' attention to the predictions. After reading each prediction, students may decide that the prediction is correct, needs to be adjusted, or needs to be completely thrown out. Before returning to the text, the teacher can ask students to share new predictions based on what they have just read. Again, after reading several more pages, students can re-examine their predictions. These two steps, making and confirming (or adjusting or rejecting) predictions, can be repeated throughout the process of reading the text. The teacher should model for students how to use this strategy before having students attempt it independently. (Standards 5.2, 7.1, 7.4)

Monitor Comprehension—
Set the Purpose

List, Group, and Label

Directions: Brainstorm some words that are related to your topic.
Then sort those words into different categories. Label each category.

Topic: _____

Label:	Label:	Label:	Label:

#50468 *Successful Strategies* © *Shell Education*

Monitor Comprehension— Set the Purpose

Word Sort

Directions: Read the words in the word bank that are related to your topic. Choose three groups to make for the words. Label the groups. Write words from the word bank in the different groups.

Topic:_____

Word bank	Group 1:	Group 2:	Group 3:

Monitor Comprehension—
Set the Purpose

Brainstorming

Directions: Write the topic in the center oval. Write a word or group of words in each outside oval that tells about the topic.

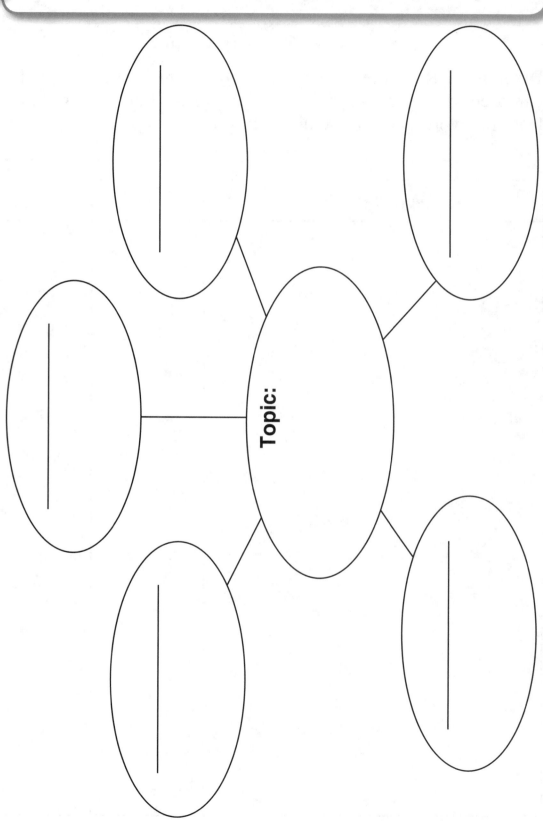

Topic:

Monitor Comprehension—
Set the Purpose

KWL Chart

What do I know? (K)	What do I want to learn? (W)	What did I learn? (L)

Monitor Comprehension— Set the Purpose

Anticipation Guide—Part 1

Directions: Before reading the text, write **yes** next to the statements with which you agree and **no** next to the statements with which you disagree. Write the reason why you agree or disagree in the space next to the statement. After reading the selection, decide whether you still agree or disagree with each statement.

Statement	Yes/No	Reason
1.		
2.		
3.		
4.		

Monitor Comprehension— Set the Purpose

Anticipation Guide—Part 2

Directions: Before reading the text, write **yes** next to the statements with which you agree and **no** next to the statements with which you disagree. Write the reason why you agree or disagree in the space below the statement. After reading the selection, decide whether you still agree or disagree with each statement.

Yes/No   Statement

_____   1. _____

_____

_____

_____   2. _____

_____

_____

_____   3. _____

_____

_____

_____   4. _____

_____

_____

_____   5. _____

_____

_____

"I Wonder" Statements

Directions: Choose a topic you are interested in learning more about. Find a nonfiction book that you think will help you learn more about this topic. Write the title of the book below. Then write six "I wonder" statements about the topic. Finally, read the nonfiction book and see if it answers your questions.

Book title: _____

1. _____

2. _____

3. _____

4. _____

5. _____

6. _____

Monitor Comprehension—
Set the Purpose

Surveying the Text

Directions: Look at the different parts of your book. Decide what you can learn from each part. Then write your purpose for reading this book.

- Table of contents

  I will learn: _____

  _____

- Preface

  I will learn: _____

  _____

- Appendix

  I will learn: _____

  _____

- Graphic features (charts, maps, diagrams, etc.)

  I will learn: _____

  _____

- Headings

  I will learn: _____

  _____

My purpose for reading this book is:_____

_____

Monitor Comprehension— Set the Purpose

Making Predictions

Directions: Read the title of your book. Look through the pages. Follow the steps below.

1. Make a prediction of what you think the book will be about.

   _____

   _____

2. Read several pages. Was your prediction correct? Is there anything you want to change?

   _____

   _____

3. Make a prediction of what you think will happen next.

   _____

   _____

4. Read several pages. Was your prediction correct? Is there anything you want to change?

   _____

   _____

5. Make a prediction of what you think will happen next.

   _____

   _____

6. Read several pages. Was your prediction correct? Is there anything you want to change?

   _____

   _____

Monitor Comprehension— Set the Purpose

Study Guide for Guided Reading

Directions: First, set your purpose for reading. Then scan the text and predict what it will tell you. Write your answers in each box.

Purpose:
Who:
What:
When:
Where:
How:

Monitor Comprehension—
Set the Purpose

Thinking About My Reading

Directions: After reading a selection, think about what you did before, during, and after reading it. Answer the following questions by putting an **X** in either the **Yes** or the **No** column.

	Yes	No
Before I read, did I look at the text?		
Did I make predictions?		
While I was reading, did I stop to think about what I was reading?		
Did I change my predictions?		
After I read, did I think back about my predictions?		
Did I summarize in my head what I read?		

I can improve my reading by _____

_____

_____

Monitor Comprehension—
Set the Purpose

Prereading Prediction

Directions: Read the title of the book. Write two sentences stating your predictions. Draw a picture of what you think this book will be about.

1. _____

_____

_____

2. _____

_____

_____

Monitor Comprehension—
Author's Point of View

Expository texts are written to give factual information about their subjects. They can be difficult for young students to comprehend because students are often unfamiliar with the structural patterns in them. Graphs, charts, diagrams, maps, and captioned illustrations are often part of expository texts. To be able to attend to the vast amount of information in expository texts, students need to slow their reading rate and look at all of the information on the page. Teachers can guide students through the text structures and teach them to be successful at comprehending the information. The teacher should introduce students to these different types of nonfiction text.

Students often believe that everything written in expository texts is true. That is not always the case. The authors' viewpoints and biases become evident through their word choices and tone. Teachers need to teach students to become discriminating readers and not to believe everything they see in print. They need to be able to determine the difference between fact and opinion and understand an author's message and relate it to their own lives. Teachers can begin to teach young students how to become critical readers through direct instruction.

When reading nonfiction, students need to be able to discern fact from opinion. To do so, they must first know the definitions of both words. A *fact* is something true that can be verified by checking another source. For example, if they read "Hawaii is in the Pacific Ocean," students can look on a map to check the accuracy of that statement. Other references for checking facts include the Internet, dictionaries, encyclopedias, etc. An *opinion* is an attitude or belief about something that is unique to the person holding that opinion. It is not verifiable. Readers cannot prove an opinion by checking other sources. An author might write, "Ducks are the most beautiful bird." That may be what the author thinks, but it is not a fact that can be checked. The reader may dislike ducks and find them unattractive. Authors often combine facts and opinion in their writing, so students need to be taught how to differentiate between the two.

Strategy 1: Key Words

One way to teach students the difference between fact and opinion is by looking at key words that signal opinions. Some of the key words that signal an opinion are *seems, believe, likely, think, probably, may,* and *appears.* Many adjectives also are a sign of opinions. These include *best, pretty,* and *biggest.* Point out these key words and adjectives when they appear in a text. Students need this knowledge to check for facts and opinions. The activity on page 44 gives students practice in identifying key words. (Standards 5.6, 7.1)

Monitor Comprehension—Author's Point of View

Strategy 2: Building Prior Knowledge—Fact or Opinion?

Since young students have had little exposure to the concepts of fact and opinion, the teacher should build prior knowledge. Having prior knowledge or experiences will help students learn to discriminate between fact and opinion. Mini-lessons can teach key words that signal opinions. On the board or overhead projector, the teacher shows a pair of statements, one with only facts, the other with opinions. The sentences should have some of the same words in them to make it easier to find the key words. The following two sentences are examples:

> Baseball is a sport that is played with a ball.

> Baseball is a boring sport.

After the teacher reads each statement, the class discusses if it is a fact or opinion. Students can identify the words that are the same in each statement (*baseball*, *sport*). Students can check the first sentence by looking up the definition of baseball in the dictionary. This research can lead to the conclusion that the first statement is a fact. If students agree with the second statement, they may also believe it is a fact. The teacher then draws their attention to the word that signals an opinion (*boring*) and explains why this statement is not a fact. Once the word has been identified, the teacher writes it on a chart that can be posted to include key words that signal opinion. The teacher writes another pair of sentences and repeats the lesson. This practice builds background knowledge of words that show opinion. This difficult concept needs modeling many times, and the teacher needs to review the chart of key words every day so students become familiar with them. The activities on pages 45 and 46 can be used to help students distinguish between fact and opinion. (Standards 5.6, 7.4)

Strategy 3: Fact and Opinion T-Chart

The teacher makes a T-chart on the board/chart paper, writing *Fact* on one side and *Opinion* on the other. Some statements can be put on chart paper or on the overhead projector. It is important that students can see the words as they are learning to be critical readers. After the teacher reads each statement, students tell whether to write it on the fact or opinion side of the T-chart. Students use a nonverbal signal to indicate their choices—an open hand for fact and a fist for opinion. They have to justify their choices, so those who may not agree can hear the thinking behind their decisions. After the statements are written on the T-chart, the teacher or a student underlines the key words that signal an opinion. The words are added to the reference chart of key words if they are not already on it. Students should refer to the chart during the activity to see if any of the words are there. After some guided practice, students can do this activity with a partner using individual T-charts and prewritten statements, cutting and pasting them on the correct side. (Standards 5.2, 5.6, 7.1, 7.4)

Strategy 4: Fact Hunt

During guided reading, students can go on a fact hunt in their guided-reading books. As students find facts, they are listed for everyone in the group to see. Simple nonfiction books with short text work well for this activity. Also, many science trade books are good to use. Facts are often presented as captions under pictures, so it makes them easier to find. Students will be eager to find the facts. As a follow-up, students choose one of the facts to write and illustrate. These facts can be put into a class book. The activity on page 47 can be used for this activity. (Standards 5.2, 5.6, 7.1)

Monitor Comprehension— Author's Point of View

Strategy 5: Highlighting

Students love to use highlighters. The teacher writes a short paragraph on chart paper and includes facts and opinions. Some of the opinions should be obvious. Using a different colored highlighter for facts and opinions, students come to the chart to highlight the text and then discuss how they decided if a statement was a fact or an opinion. (Standard 7.4)

Strategy 6: Roll the Cube

Reinforcing the strategies above through a game is a motivating way for students to practice skills. Before reproducing the dice pattern on page 48, write "fact" or "opinion" in each box, and then make copies for the students. Students cut out the pattern on their copies and put the cube together. Next, they roll the cube and state either a "fact" or an "opinion," depending on what they rolled. They can use the T-chart developed in an earlier lesson for their statements. Or, the teacher might have a chart of newly learned facts in a social studies lesson, and they can use those as facts. They can try to change the facts to opinions by inserting a key word from the reference chart. Another way to use the cube is to write several facts and opinions from a recent lesson on each side of the cube. After students roll the die, they read the statement and decide if it is a fact or an opinion. (Standards 5.2, 7.4, 8.2)

Strategy 7: News Flash!

Student newspapers are great sources of facts and opinions. During guided reading, the class reads an article in the newspaper. Students pick out statements that are facts. They copy one statement onto the activity titled "News Flash!" on page 49 and illustrate it. The teacher can also bring in sections of a newspaper and work on finding facts and opinions together. Students can again choose a fact to write and illustrate on the activity. The finished activities can be displayed on a bulletin board or in a class book of "Fantastic Facts." (Standards 5.2, 5.6, 7.1)

Strategy 8: What's the Purpose?

Young students tend to think that everything in the newspaper is true. Teachers can use parts of a newspaper to demonstrate different purposes for writing in guided-reading groups. The class works on one section at a time, discussing it and determining the author's purpose for writing. After each section has been read and discussed, students and teacher can determine the author's purpose. Using a large poster that is divided into four different author's purposes, students can glue the newspaper section under the appropriate heading. Parts of the newspaper that can be used include TV listings, the weather section, advertisements, and the sports page. The activity on page 50 can be used for this activity. (Standards 5.2, 7.1, 8.2, 8.5)

Strategy 9: The Daily News

After students have some experience writing the news as a group, they can complete a similar activity independently or in pairs. Students can use The Daily News activity on page 51 to make individual or small-group newspapers. All of the newspapers can be available as reading material for the class. (Standards 7.1, 8.5)

Monitor Comprehension— Author's Point of View

Strategy 10: Point of View

After hearing and reading selections in first- and third-person points of view, students can practice writing in both. Students should have previously participated in many guided-writing lessons where both types of writing were modeled. This activity should be done in small groups. Half of the class can write in third person and the other half in first person. The teacher gives students a picture that relates to a subject they have been learning about. Students who are writing in third person do not use first-person pronouns such as *I*, *me*, *we*, or *my* in their writing. Students who are writing in first person should begin by drawing themselves and then write from that perspective. The Point of View activity on page 52 can be used for this strategy. Pictures can be attached to the template and copied. The following is how the writing may look. (Standards 5.1, 5.2, 7.4)

First-person point of view: I planted a seed. It will grow into a plant. I put the seed in the dirt. Then I will water the seed. I will put it in the sun. My plant will grow a flower and leaves.

Third-person point of view: All plants grow from seeds. They grow into different kinds of plants. Plants need sun, water, and soil to grow. Plants have leaves and stems.

Strategy 11: Role-Playing

After learning about famous people in social studies, each student can write short paragraphs from the point of view of a famous person. (Standards 5.2, 7.2, 7.3)

Strategy 12: What's the News?

Students can work in groups to write the daily class news. Each group should have markers and chart paper to record the news. The news might include the weather, classroom activities, playground happenings, the lunch menu, etc. Students love to talk about the day, and using the markers and chart paper is motivating for them. News items are usually a mix of first- and third-person accounts. When the groups are done writing, one person from each group uses a fake microphone and reports the news. Students can identify point of view in some of the news. (Standard 8.5)

Strategy 13: Stump Your Partner

Using the activity on page 53, play the Stump Your Partner game. Students write their own facts and opinions and exchange papers with partners. Each partner has to read the other's statements and determine if they are fact or opinion. Encourage students to use key words in their opinions and see if they can trick or stump their partners. Check their work to ensure its accuracy and avoid any conflicts of student opinion. (Standards 7.4, 8.2, 8.5)

Monitor Comprehension— Author's Point of View

Strategy 14: What's the Problem?

Students need to understand that authors often include their own beliefs in their writing. They don't always show that there are two sides to an issue. This stance is called *bias*. Teachers can help students understand bias by presenting it in ways they understand, such as student conflict. Teachers can use pictures of students having problems. Examples include the following: one student has a handful of crayons and the other student has her empty hand outstretched; a student is on the playground crying and another student is standing near him; and two students are playing a board game, both look angry, and one is pointing at the board. Using the pictures for discussion, the teacher pairs students and has each one role-play one of the students in the picture. Each student tells his or her side of the disagreement. Teachers guide students to see that the problem is dependent on who tells the story. The activity on page 54 provides situations for discussion.

Authors write for different reasons. Readers need to be able to figure out the message that the author is trying to send, the tone in which it was written, and the validity of the point of view. Teachers can begin teaching young students how to become critical readers. They need to learn to reread to check the accuracy of information. Students also need to learn to differentiate between fact and opinion. Teachers can present this information through explicit guided lessons. Students can begin to learn how to use the structure of nonfiction texts to recognize themes. This guided practice establishes the prior knowledge young students need as they move through the grade levels and become critical readers. (Standards 5.1, 5.2, 7.3, 7.4, 8.2)

Strategy 15: First Person/Third Person

After students have read or heard selections written from both the first-person and the third-person points of view, give them writing prompts to complete during guided writing. Have some prompts use first person and some use third person so students have experience writing from both viewpoints. As students become more accomplished at this task, split up the class and have half write from first person and half write in third person.

Use the activity on page 55 to partner students and have them either write both viewpoints together or each write a different viewpoint (first person/third person). Post these on a bulletin board or place them in a class book so students can read both viewpoints side by side. (Students 5.2, 7.4, 8.5)

Strategy 16: Figure It Out

Generate a list of themes or messages that are common to nonfiction texts. You can create this list as a class, or you can do it and post it for your class. (Examples: working together, having an adventure, helping others, survival, etc.) As you read stories aloud to students, discuss possible messages the author is trying to convey. Discuss how to determine the message by using text events. As a class, decide on two hints that the author gives about his or her message. Use the activity on pages 56 and 57 to work with students on this strategy. (Standards 5.1, 5.2, 7.2, 7.4)

Monitor Comprehension—
Author's Point of View

Strategy 17: Connecting My Reading to My Life

Have students relate the author's message or theme to something in their own lives. By connecting the message to an event in their lives, students will be more successful in understanding the author's purpose for writing. Use the activity on page 58 as guided or independent practice. (Standards 5.1, 5.2, 7.4)

Strategy 18: Author Awareness

Use many types of texts to show students the different reasons authors have for writing. Use ads, narratives, descriptions, etc. Have students read the text and discuss why they think the author wrote it. Students often think that because it is in writing, it is true. They don't understand that people use print to try to sell things or convince readers that one thing is right or better than another. By exposing students to various types of writing and discussing the authors' reasons for writing, students become aware of different purposes for writing. (Standards 7.1, 7.2, 8.5)

Strategy 19: My Side/Your Side

Give students the activity on page 59, partner students together, and have each of them choose one side of a problem. Students discuss the problem and write both sides on the same page, next to each other. Read them aloud or post them in the classroom for other students to read to see which side they agree with. (Standard 7.2)

Strategy 20: Agree or Disagree?

Students also need to learn that they can disagree with the text or with what the author has written. By reading aloud and having students read sections, discuss if they agree or disagree with the author. Find or write selections relevant to the students such as "Dogs Are Better Than Cats" or "Monday Is the Best Day of the Week."

After reading, discuss how they could tell that the author's personal belief was included or that it was a one-sided selection. Using examples that students can understand will clearly illustrate that there can be two sides; however, authors often don't show opposing viewpoints. Use the activity on page 60 as independent practice to have students respond to texts by agreeing or disagreeing.

Teaching students to read critically and discriminatingly can begin in the first and second grades. Teachers will introduce skills that students will continue to develop for the rest of their lives as readers. Nonfiction texts offer many opportunities to teach students how to become critical readers. Instructing students to differentiate between fact and opinion, look at the author's use of structure and viewpoint, and begin to find the messages or themes in texts will teach students to become critical readers. (Standard 7.2)

Monitor Comprehension— Author's Point of View

Key Words

Directions: The sentences below are all opinions. Underline the key word or words in each sentence that lets you know they are opinions.

1. Summer is the best season.

2. The park is a really fun place to play.

3. Big dogs are better than small dogs.

4. Soccer is more fun than football.

Directions: Write a sentence that is an opinion. Underline the key word you used.

_____

_____

_____

Monitor Comprehension— Author's Point of View

Building Prior Knowledge—Fact or Opinion?

Directions: Read each sentence. If it is a fact, write an **F** on the line. If it is an opinion, write an **O**.

_____ 1. The moon is covered with craters.

_____ 2. Snakes are scary animals.

_____ 3. Chocolate ice cream is the best.

_____ 4. Dinosaurs are extinct.

_____ 5. Zebras have black and white stripes.

_____ 6. Red cars are pretty.

Monitor Comprehension— Author's Point of View

Building Prior Knowledge—Fact or Opinion?

Directions: Underline the words in the following statements that let you know they are opinions. Key words can help you determine the difference between a fact and an opinion.

1. Carrots are the best vegetable.

2. Dogs are better pets than cats.

3. P. E. will probably be boring today.

4. Baseball is the best sport.

5. I believe the Dallas Cowboys will win the Super Bowl this year.

6. Pizza from the cafeteria is really tasty.

Write two sentences that are opinions. Make sure you include key words in each sentence.

1. _____

_____

_____

_____

2. _____

_____

_____

_____

Monitor Comprehension— Author's Point of View

Fact Hunt

Directions: Write the title of your book. Then write two facts that you read in your book. On the back of this page, draw a picture of each. Remember: A *fact* is something that is true. An *opinion* is how you feel about something.

Title:_____

1. _____

   _____

2. _____

   _____

What do you think about the book? Write your opinion of the book.

_____

_____

_____

_____

_____

_____

_____

Monitor Comprehension—Author's Point of View

Roll the Cube

Directions: Cut out the cube and use it to play the fact or opinion game.

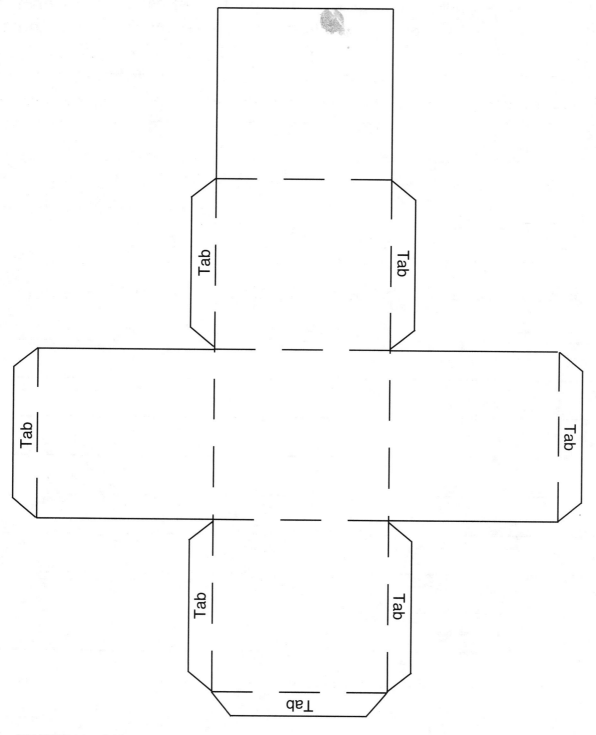

Monitor Comprehension—Author's Point of View

News Flash!

Directions: Write a fact that you read in your newspaper. Draw a picture of it.

News fact: _____

_____

_____

_____

_____

Monitor Comprehension— Author's Point of View

What's the Purpose?

Directions: Write your topic below. Then find and write the author's purpose. Explain how you know.

Topic: _____

The author's purpose is _____

_____

_____

_____

_____

_____ .

I know this because _____

_____

_____

_____

_____

_____

_____

_____ .

Monitor Comprehension—
Author's Point of View

The Daily News

Directions: Write the news for today. It can be about home, school, family, or friends. Draw pictures to go with the news.

_____ **Daily News**

Monitor Comprehension—
Author's Point of View

Point of View

Directions: Look at the picture. Write about it using the _____ person point of view.

Monitor Comprehension—
Author's Point of View

Stump Your Partner

Directions: Write five statements. Make sure some are facts and some are opinions. Have your partner read them and write an **O** on the line if the statement is an opinion or an **F** on the line if the statement is a fact.

_____ 1. _____

_____

_____

_____ 2. _____

_____

_____

_____ 3. _____

_____

_____

_____ 4. _____

_____

_____

_____ 5. _____

_____

_____

Monitor Comprehension— Author's Point of View

What's the Problem?

Directions: Use the cards for discussion. Tell about the problems in the pictures from different points of view.

Monitor Comprehension— Author's Point of View

First Person/Third Person

Directions: With a partner, write two responses to the prompt. Use the first-person point of view for one response and the third-person point of view for the other response.

Prompt: _____

First person	Third person

Monitor Comprehension— Author's Point of View

Figure It Out

Directions: What is the author's message? Fill in the boxes using your book and the hints you decide upon as a class.

Hint: _____

_____

Hint: _____

_____

Using these hints, I think the author is trying to say . . .

_____

_____

_____

_____

_____

_____

_____

_____

_____

_____

Monitor Comprehension— Author's Point of View

Figure It Out *(cont.)*

Topic: _____

Author's message:

_____

_____

_____

_____

_____

I know this because . . .

_____

_____

_____

_____

_____

Monitor Comprehension— Author's Point of View

Connecting My Reading to My Life

Title: _____

Author's message: _____

_____

This reminds me of _____

_____

_____

_____

_____

_____

Illustration:

Monitor Comprehension—Author's Point of View

My Side/Your Side

Directions: With a partner, write arguments for both sides of the topic. You can each write one side of the topic, or you can write both sides together.

Topic: _____

My side	Your side
_____	_____
_____	_____
_____	_____
_____	_____
_____	_____
_____	_____
_____	_____
_____	_____
_____	_____
_____	_____

Monitor Comprehension— Author's Point of View

Agree or Disagree?

Topic: _____

Do you agree or disagree with the author? Circle one.

Agree   **Disagree**

Support your choice with three reasons.

1. _____

   _____

   _____

2. _____

   _____

   _____

3. _____

   _____

   _____

PASSPORT TO COMPREHENSION

Activate
and
Connect

#50468 Successful Strategies

Activate and Connect

Teaching comprehension to students requires teachers to build on students' prior knowledge. Prior knowledge is information or experiences that students bring to a lesson. Research has shown that there is a relationship between prior knowledge and comprehension. Making connections between this prior knowledge and new information enhances comprehension. As students have more experiences, they add more information to the cognitive structure of knowledge in their minds. As new information is introduced, students compare it to what they already know. It is similar to having a filing system and looking for the file containing the information you need.

Students need to have a purpose for reading. Activating and developing prior knowledge can create this purpose. Using prior knowledge enables students to construct meaning. Students come to school with varying degrees and amounts of prior knowledge. Some students have incomplete or incorrect prior knowledge. The teacher must assess the students' prior knowledge. While the teacher is assessing, he or she is also activating prior knowledge. After assessment, the teacher may be able to change incorrect information and enhance learning. When teachers ask students to make connections and tell what they think, the students' levels of interest increase. They are likely to think more carefully.

There are two ways to think about prior knowledge: overall prior knowledge, and text- or topic-specific prior knowledge. Overall prior knowledge is the whole of prior knowledge that students have as a result of experiences both in school and out of school. This prior knowledge is built as students read and write—activities that help increase comprehension. Text-specific or topic-specific prior knowledge is the specific information needed for a specific experience, such as having some knowledge about polar bears before reading about them.

Nonfiction texts are organized differently than narrative texts. Information in nonfiction texts is organized around main ideas. These texts are more difficult for first-graders because they have had less experience with them, and these texts usually are not patterned. Background knowledge for these texts can be built through mini-lessons and reading. The students also need to build prior knowledge about the vocabulary and the way information is presented in nonfiction texts. Holmes and Roser (1987) identified five methods for assessing prior knowledge:

1. **Free recall**

    The teacher asks students to tell what they know about a specific topic: "What do you know about _____?"

2. **Recognition**

    The teacher presents a list of words and asks students which words they think are related to the book they are about to read. The teacher writes the words *penguin*, *iceberg*, *hot weather*, *green grass*, *snow*, and *South Pole* on the board and says, "We are going to read a book about penguins. Which of these words are about penguins?"

3. **Structured questions**

    The teacher asks students prepared questions about the students' prior knowledge: "What do you know about Abraham Lincoln? What group of people did he help?"

Activate and Connect

4. **Word association**

   The teacher shares a list of words and asks students what they think of when they hear them: "When I say *leaves*, *stems*, and *seeds*, what do you think I'm talking about?"

5. **Unstructured discussion**

   The teacher asks open-ended questions about the topic: "We are going to read about volcanoes. What do you know about them?"

The teacher's goal is to help students make connections between prior knowledge and new information. Students need to become independent in accessing and using their prior knowledge. In primary grades, the teacher should model many different strategies for making connections. The strategies can be used one at a time or several together. These opportunities will build the foundation for students to become independent in activating prior knowledge in later grades.

When activating knowledge, there are three kinds of connections students can make between the new information and prior experiences:

1. **Text to self:** Students compare and relate the information in the new text to some experience they have had at some other time in their lives.

2. **Text to text:** Students compare the information in the new text to other books that they may have already read.

3. **Text to world:** Students compare and relate the information in the new text to world events.

The easiest connections to make are between text and self. Young students love to tell about things they know, did, etc. The connection between text and self is the one to begin with; the teacher can then move to text-to-text connections. The most difficult, especially for young students, are text-to-world connections, so these should be the last ones to use.

When choosing strategies to use for activating prior knowledge, it is important for the teacher to review the text and think about the prior knowledge that needs to be activated and which strategies will fulfill this goal. Teachers must decide what they want students to accomplish in connection with the topic and what the big concepts are that students need to understand. Knowing these concepts will help teachers determine the prior knowledge that is most likely to help students understand the text.

Activate and Connect

Strategy 1: My Book and Me—Picture/Text Walk

Text walk is a strategy that many primary teachers use during guided reading. It is a very structured strategy and should always be teacher-led. This method helps readers develop main ideas, vocabulary, and an overall picture of the text before reading. In a picture/text walk, the teacher guides students through the text and pictures, focusing on key ideas and vocabulary that help students make connections to prior knowledge. The teacher needs to read the text before introducing it to students so that he or she is familiar with the vocabulary and key ideas. The My Book and Me activity on page 72 helps students write and draw what they saw in the picture/text walk. Students also write what they are reminded of, making a connection between text and self. (Standards 5.2, 7.4, 8.2, 8.5)

Strategy 2: Preview and Predict

Before reading a nonfiction book, students should look at the book cover, read the title, and look at the pictures to get an idea of what they think they will learn. Using prior knowledge and the information from the preview, students predict what they will learn. The teacher may want to read captions under pictures as part of the previewing. In the early grades, the previewing and predicting should be kept simple. After previewing and predicting, students read the text and check their predictions. They change or keep their predictions as needed after reading. Teachers need to remind students that they will be thinking the whole time they are reading. This sets a purpose for reading. The teacher must model the procedure and guide young students through it so that they understand and learn how to use the strategy. This strategy is best used when students have some knowledge of the topic. The activity on page 73 can be used for previewing and predicting. (Standards 5.2, 7.4)

Strategy 3: Prove It

This prediction strategy works well with nonfiction texts. Students make predictions based on the title and book cover. The teacher writes the predictions on the board and numbers them. Then students preview the section of the book the class will be working on that day. The teacher should limit the amount of time allowed for looking at the section so the faster readers do not read all of the text. Students should make predictions based on captions, charts, and pictures and then read the previewed section. After reading, students share which predictions were true and which were not. To "prove it," they should find the text to back up their claims. The teacher puts a check mark by the true predictions and crosses out or modifies any false predictions. At the end, the teacher asks students to share the important things that they learned that they could not predict from the pictures. The activity on page 74 provides practice with this strategy. (Standards 5.2, 8.2, 8.5)

Activate and Connect

Strategy 4: Brainstorming

When brainstorming, students tell all they know about a topic, thereby activating their prior knowledge. Students must have some prior knowledge about the topic to use this strategy. Brainstorming should be done in a whole group because students can listen as others share, and a whole-group setting usually encourages more students to share. The teacher writes the topic on the board or chart paper and asks students to provide any information they have about the topic. On the board, the teacher writes the information students give under the topic. If wrong information is given, the teacher can also write it down. It can be discussed and corrected after reading the text. The teacher may have to prompt students by asking questions that activate prior knowledge. Later, students can begin to use this strategy in pairs or groups. They can work together to record their information. They should still share it in a whole group so the teacher can record the information on a class chart. It is also important for all groups to see the different responses. Brainstorming is an effective way to assess prior knowledge. The template on page 75 can assist students with brainstorming. (Standards 7.4, 8.2)

Strategy 5: KWL Chart

A KWL chart requires students to focus on two questions before reading and one question after reading. Students set a purpose for reading by thinking about what they already know (K) about a topic and what they want to learn (W). After reading, they think about what they did learn (L). In early grades, this strategy is best used in a large-group setting. Students need guidance and modeling with this strategy. The teacher draws a KWL chart on the board; as students share information for each section, the teacher records it. The following is a brief outline of the steps:

Step 1: What do I know? (K) The teacher introduces the topic and students brainstorm what they already know about the subject. The teacher may need to ask questions to help students activate prior knowledge.

Step 2: What do I want to learn? (W) As students share information that they already know, it may prompt questions about things they would like to know. These questions are recorded in the W section of the chart and are used to focus students' reading. They should be looking for answers to their questions as they read.

Step 3: What did I learn? (L) After reading, students answer the questions they posed before reading. They can also see which questions they may not have found answers for, establishing a purpose to read more on the subject.

After students have had many opportunities to work with KWL charts in a whole-group setting, they can work together in pairs or small groups to fill out individual forms. The information on these forms should be shared with the whole group and posted for all to see. Activities using KWL charts can be found on pages 76 and 77. A variation of the KWL chart that some young students may be able to use, depending on their abilities, is the Nonfiction Story Map on page 78. In the early grades, such an activity should include an area for students to draw pictures of their responses if they cannot express all of their learning through words. (Standards 5.2, 7.4, 8.2)

Activate and Connect

Strategy 6: Rivet

The game of Rivet is another activity that uses predictions. It is a game similar to Hangman. The teacher picks four to eight important words that are going to be read in the chosen text. He or she draws lines on the board, one for each letter in the word and then for all the words. The words should be numbered. The teacher writes the letters in for each word, one at a time, and gives students a chance to try to guess the word. When a student guesses the word, the teacher finishes filling in the letters. Students may not be able to guess the difficult words, but they will still be watching the teacher write in the letters and trying to guess. Their eyes should be "riveted" to the board. When all the words are written, students use as many of the words as possible to make predictions about what the book will be about. The teacher writes their predictions on the board. After reading the selection, the class goes over the predictions and checks which ones actually happened. Students love to play games, and when predictions and vocabulary are presented in this way, students will be engaged in their learning. (Standards 5.2, 5.6, 8.5)

Strategy 7: Quick Write/Quick Draw

Quick write/quick draw is an independent strategy that can be linked to brainstorming. Each student has an index card. The large ones are better for young students. The teacher gives students five to ten minutes to write and draw anything they know about the subject of the book. Having the option to write or draw is important for young students. Some express themselves much better through illustrations. When the time is up, students share by telling what they have written or sharing what they have drawn. The information shared can be recorded on the board or chart as done in brainstorming. After discussion, students and teacher read the text. As they read, students should be looking for new things about the topic. When reading is completed, students write or draw two or three things they learned on the back of their index cards. They can share what they learned when they are done. Writing and drawing activities allow all students to participate and help set a purpose for reading. (Standards 5.2, 7.4)

Strategy 8: Reading Aloud

Reading aloud is an excellent strategy to use when students have limited background knowledge about a topic. The teacher can introduce a topic through a read-aloud. Before reading a book on the topic, the teacher can show students a collection of nonfiction books that will be available for reading about the topic. These can help motivate students and activate their interest in a new topic. The teacher can read aloud one of the books about the topic to build background knowledge before students read other books about the topic. Students need a purpose for learning. Teachers may want them to listen for main ideas or new words. Read-aloud can be paired with predicting. After the read-aloud, students discuss what was learned. (Standard 7.4)

Activate and Connect

Strategy 9: Compare and Contrast—Venn Diagram

As students are exposed to more books, they can compare them to other books that they have already read. They can also compare the information in nonfiction books with what they might have learned from doing things outside of school. Comparing and contrasting are great ways to activate this prior knowledge. The teacher can teach this strategy by comparing a new book to one that students read earlier. This instruction should be explicit. The teacher cannot just assume students will connect the new book to the previous one. With this information, students are ready to read the new book. Similarities are easier for young students to see. The teacher should also point out differences between books. The information can be shared with students by drawing a Venn diagram on the board and filling it in together. For example, if students are learning about different foods, they may compare an apple to a tomato. Some similarities that students may point out are that both are red, both are good for you, and both are round. Some differences they may see are that the apple grows on a tree while the tomato grows on a leafy plant, and the apple is crunchy while the tomato is soft. The teacher will need to ask questions and guide students to see the differences. Students in pairs can fill in small Venn diagrams to compare and contrast. The ideas or objects that they are comparing need to be objects that are familiar to them. It is too difficult for them to compare and contrast complex ideas. A template for a Venn diagram is provided on page 79. (Standards 7.4, 8.2, 8.5)

Strategy 10: Preview and Self-Question

A variation of preview and predict that can be used with nonfiction texts is preview and self-question. As in preview and predict, students look at the title of the book, the illustrations, and any margin notes or captions before reading. But instead of making predictions about the text, students will ask questions that they think will be answered by their reading. Students could use this strategy independently after several modeled lessons.

Example:

Teacher: I am going to read a book about sea turtles. I'll look at the cover, the illustrations, and the captions before I begin reading to see what I may learn from reading this book.

(Teacher does this in front of the class, reading aloud the captions and any other necessary information.)

Teacher: As I read this book, I think I am going to find the answers to some questions I have about sea turtles. I am going to write down my questions so I remember them as I read.

(Teacher writes "What do sea turtles eat? Where do sea turtles live?" on the board or on a chart.)

Teacher: Now I am ready to read my book. I hope I find the answers to my questions. You can help me by giving a thumbs-up when you hear the answers to my questions.

(Teacher reads the book aloud to the class, and students signal when the book answers the questions.)

Activate and Connect

Strategy 10: Preview and Self-Question *(cont.)*

This strategy can also be used when reading a nonfiction article or a single chapter from a book. After modeling the strategy several times, students will be able to try it on their own. The teacher can provide a book or an article and lead students through the process. Students can do the previewing on their own and then write down one or two questions that they think the reading will answer. As the year progresses and students become familiar with this strategy, the teacher can require students to ask more questions prior to reading. The activity on page 80 helps students write their own questions. (Standards 5.2, 7.1, 8.2)

Strategy 11: Visualizing

Many nonfiction books use comparisons, captions, charts, and diagrams to present information. These nonfiction conventions are often interesting to students and capture their interest. The teacher should build background knowledge of these conventions by introducing one convention at a time. Comparisons are used frequently to describe size, length, distance, and weight. The comparisons are usually ones that young students are familiar with. Making comparisons helps students visualize difficult concepts, such as the size of a blue whale's tongue. If a measurement is given without a comparison, the numbers hold little significance for students. But when they read that a blue whale's tongue is as big as a car, they have a point of reference to compare to the tongue. The teacher and students can search through books for conventions, and as they learn about them, the teacher can record them on a class chart. Students can record the conventions in individual convention journals. Using the conventions to visualize information that may otherwise be abstract supports students' comprehension of nonfiction texts. (Standards 5.1, 5.2, 7.1)

Activate and Connect

Strategy 12: Anticipation Guides

Anticipation guides are statements made about the text that students are going to read. They can be used to create a link between students' prior knowledge and what they will learn from reading the text. They are also a good strategy to use when students are not familiar with the topic. Readence, Bean, and Baldwin (1998) established a set of guidelines to activate students' prior knowledge through the use of anticipation guides. Following these steps will help the teacher make and use these guides successfully in the classroom:

Step 1—Review the text to determine the key concepts.

Step 2—Identify students' prior knowledge. Using your knowledge of your students, figure out what they probably already know.

Step 3—Create statements. Using the information in the first two steps, write out statements about the text for students to read and decide whether they agree or disagree with them. The statements should be related to the concepts in the text and can contain information about which students do not have any prior knowledge. The number of statements you create will depend on the length of the text. You will probably want to write between four and eight statements. At the first- and second-grade levels, you will probably want to start with true/false statements. As students become more familiar with this strategy, don't limit yourself to only this type of statement.

Step 4—Determine how you will present the statements and the order in which they will be presented. The statement order should follow the order of the text. Determine if you will present it to the entire group on the overhead or the board, or if students will individually receive the statements during an activity.

Step 5—Present the statements. The class will read and respond to each statement by agreeing or disagreeing with it. You may have them share their responses with the group.

Step 6—Discuss the statements. As a group, discuss the statements and why students agree or disagree with them. You may consider making a group tally next to each statement.

Step 7—Read the text. Have your class read the text, thinking about the statements they have just seen and discussed.

Step 8—Follow up. Complete the rest of the guide by rereading the statements and using the information learned in the text to now agree or disagree.

Activate and Connect

Strategy 12: Anticipation Guides *(cont.)*

The following is an example of how the steps might look in context:

Your class is going to be reading a book about American holidays. The teacher reads through the article and determines the key concepts and decides approximately how much the class already knows about the holidays discussed (Steps 1 and 2). Next, the teacher writes four to eight true or false statements about the text. For example, President's Day is a holiday celebrating two famous American presidents, George Washington and Abraham Lincoln. Memorial Day is a holiday when we remember American people who fought in wars (Step 3). Present the statements to the class on an overhead projector. Have students signal you with a thumbs up or thumbs down as to whether they agree or disagree. Discuss their responses (Steps 4, 5, and 6). The class reads the text to themselves. When they are done, you reread the overhead statements and have them agree or disagree using the information they have just read (Steps 7 and 8).

Anticipation guides are challenging tools to use in the classroom. They require students to think about things they don't already know. But as with any strategy, as students are exposed to it and see it modeled frequently, they will become more comfortable using it.

Teachers can use the Anticipation Guide activity on page 81 for students to use independently before and after their reading. However, prior to copying the activity, the teacher must write in four statements about the text. (Standards 5.2, 5.7, 7.2, 7.4)

Strategy 13: Concrete Materials and Real Experiences

Concrete materials and real experiences are great strategies to build prior knowledge rather than activate it. Students tend to comprehend things that they can see, touch, and do. The teacher needs to clearly link the experiences to instruction and not expect students to create connections independently. Concrete materials and experiences can include field trips, videos, pictures, real objects, and experiments. If students are learning about plants and how they grow, an experiment involving different plants receiving different care can be done. (Standard 7.4)

Strategy 14: Sticky Note Sort

Sometimes background knowledge for a subject or topic needs to be built with explicit teacher instruction. Using sticky notes while reading unfamiliar texts can help the teacher and students focus on the most important information in a book. To use this method, start by gathering many books on the chosen topic. The teacher reads them and discusses the pictures and photos. As they are reading, the teacher and students write questions on sticky notes and place them on a chart. After reading several books and writing their questions on sticky notes, the teacher and students work together to sort the notes into categories. For example, if the class is learning about a pond habitat, they may have questions about animals, plants, what the animals eat, and how the animals grow. After the notes are sorted and have been discussed, students can write and draw what they have learned. (Standards 5.2, 7.1, 7.4, 8.2)

Activate and Connect

My Book and Me—Picture/Text Walk

Directions: On the left side of the book, write words or draw a picture from your book. On the right side of the book, write or draw what the words or pictures remind you of.

Activate and Connect

Preview and Predict

Directions: Write the title of the book you are going to read below. Draw the cover of the book.

Title:_____

_____

Predict: What do you think you will learn?

I predict that I will learn _____

_____

_____

_____

_____

Activate and Connect

Prove It

Directions: Before reading, fill in the left column of the chart. After reading, fill in the right column.

Book title: _____

Before reading	After reading

I predict I will learn:
 	
1. _____
 	
  _____
 	
  _____
 	
2. _____
 	
  _____
 	
  _____
 	
3. _____
 	
  _____
 	
  _____
	This is what I learned in the book:
	
	1. _____
	
	  _____
	
	  _____
	
	2. _____
	
	  _____
	
	  _____
	
	3. _____
	
	  _____
	
	  _____

Activate and Connect

Brainstorming

Directions: Write the title of your book in the center of the web. Write down what you already know about the topic of the book in the ovals.

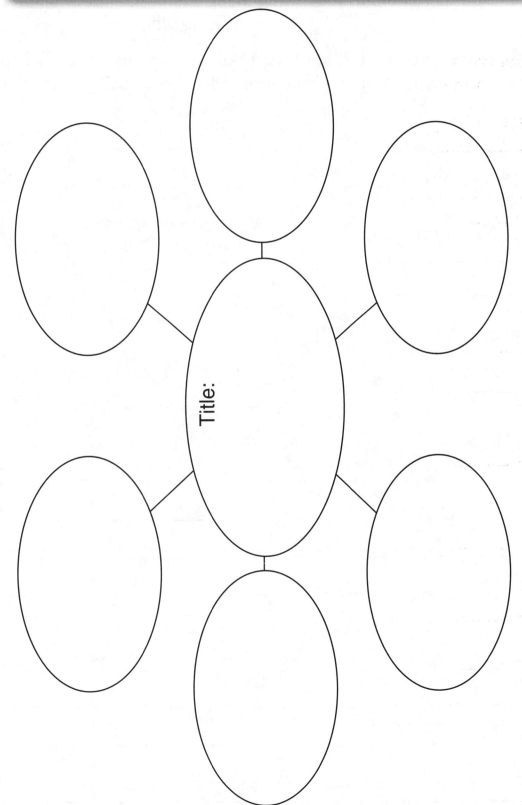

Title:

Activate and Connect

KWL Chart

Directions: Write the title of the book you are going to read. Write the book's topic. Fill in the K and W sections before you read your book. Fill in the L section with what you learned after reading.

Title:_____

Topic:_____

K: What do I know?	W: What do I want to know?	L: What did I learn?
_____	_____	_____
_____	_____	_____
_____	_____	_____
_____	_____	_____
_____	_____	_____
_____	_____	_____
_____	_____	_____
_____	_____	_____
_____	_____	_____
_____	_____	_____
_____	_____	_____
_____	_____	_____

Activate and Connect

KWL Variation

Directions: Write the title and topic of the book. Then follow the directions in each box.

Title: _____

Topic: _____

What do you already know about this topic before reading this book?

1. _____

   _____

2. _____

   _____

What do you want to know about this topic from reading this book?

1. _____

   _____

2. _____

   _____

Draw a picture and label one thing you learned from your reading on the back of this paper.

Write two questions you have about the topic that weren't answered in this book.

1. _____

   _____

2. _____

   _____

Activate and Connect

Nonfiction Story Map

Directions: Write the title of your book. The topic is what the story is about. Write the topic. Fill in the first two sections before you read the book. Fill in the last section after you finish reading. Use the boxes to draw pictures that go with your responses.

Title:_____

Topic:_____

Before reading, I knew: _____

I want to know: _____

This is what I learned: _____

Compare and Contrast—Venn Diagram

Directions: On the lines below, write the two things being compared and contrasted. Use the diagram to record their similarities and differences.

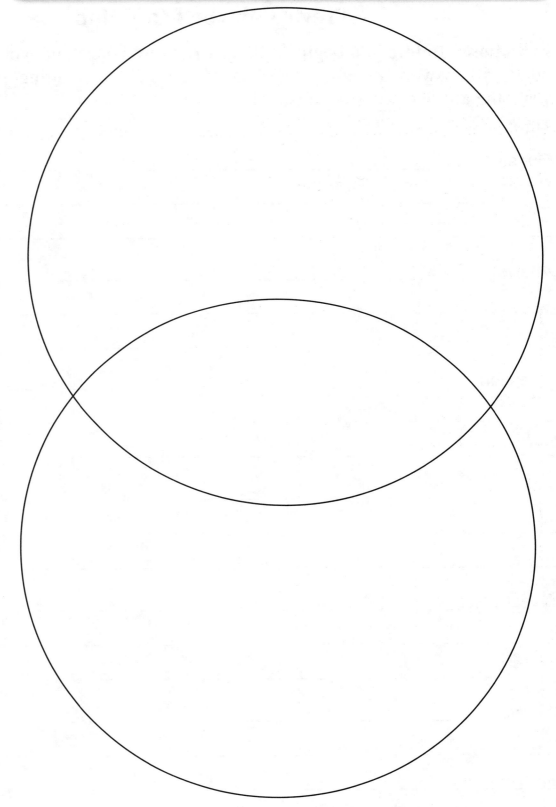

Activate and Connect

Preview and Self-Question

Directions: Before you begin reading, write three questions you think the book will answer as you read. When you are finished reading, go back and write the answers to your questions.

Title: _____

Question 1: _____

_____

_____

Answer: _____

_____

_____

Question 2: _____

_____

_____

Answer: _____

_____

_____

Question 3: _____

_____

_____

Answer: _____

_____

_____

Activate and Connect

Anticipation Guide

Directions: Read each sentence. Predict if it is true or false. Then write a **T** or **F** in each of the boxes under the "Before Reading" column. Fill in your answers before you read. After you read, reread each sentence below. Write your answers in the "After Reading" column if your predictions have changed.

Title: _____

Topic: _____

Before Reading	After Reading	
☐	☐	1. _____
☐	☐	2. _____
☐	☐	3. _____
☐	☐	4. _____

Notes

Infer Meaning

PASSPORT TO COMPREHENSION

Infer Meaning

Inferring is the ability to "read between the lines" to reach conclusions about the information presented in the text. Like detective work, inferring is taking known information and combining it with the clues or facts presented in the text. Through this process, students are then able to make a reasonable conclusion about the information being presented.

Students need to develop not only their literal-meaning comprehension skills, but also their inferential thinking skills in order to facilitate the reading and understanding of nonfiction texts. Students with strongly developed critical thinking skills are able to separate their own observations from their conclusions. These students look beyond the facts to see the implications (or the results) of the facts. Students' interpretations are based upon their own inferences.

According to Susan Hall (Harvey 1998), "Inferring allows students to make their own discoveries without the direct comment of the author." To develop comprehension and understanding of the topic, students must be able to "read between the lines" to find the underlying themes and identify the main points of the text. Making inferences, examining implied meaning, and making conclusions all require students to move beyond the literal meaning of the text and graphics by connecting their prior knowledge and experiences to the information presented in the text. Through the use of inference, students are able to make discoveries in the text they are reading.

Researchers believe that students should begin being taught how to make inferences in the primary grades (Robb 2000). Current findings indicate that being able to make reasonable and logical inferences is an important skill that can and should be developed in classroom literacy programs (Harvey 1998).

Making Different Kinds of Inferences

According to Tarasoff (1993), inferences are not limited to answering who, what, where, when, why, or how questions. Inferences can also be made regarding:

- **Location**

  Example: Mom sat in a chair to get a haircut.

  Inference: Mom is at a beauty salon.

- **Time**

  Example: We went to the circus after dinner.

  Inference: The circus started in the evening.

- **Action**

  Example: The bowler walked up to the lane and was ready to take his turn.

  Inference: The bowler is getting ready to roll the ball down the lane.

Infer Meaning

Making Different Kinds of Inferences *(cont.)*

- **Instrument**

  Example: Mom wanted Robert to stop banging so loudly.

  Inference: Robert is noisily playing the drums.

- **Object**

  Example: The sky was full of fireworks.

  Inference: There was a special celebration.

- **Category**

  Example: The boots, coats, hats, and umbrellas were dripping on the floor.

  Inference: Somebody was wearing rain gear and took it off.

- **Occupation or Pastime (Hobby)**

  Example: His job was to wash and wax all of the cars that came through.

  Inference: The person worked at a car wash.

- **Cause and Effect**

  Example: The snow made the roof cave in.

  Inference: There was a huge amount of snow on the roof.

- **Problem-Solution**

  Example: Chrissy stayed up late last night, and now we are paying for it.

  Inference: Chrissy is in a cranky mood.

- **Feeling and Attitude**

  Example: Elizabeth beamed when she received the principal's award.

  Inference: Elizabeth is proud of herself.

Making Inferences and Providing the Supporting Evidence

Anne Goudvis defines an inference as "an educated guess that comes from the blending of new information from the text with one's prior knowledge in order to make a judgment" (Harvey 1998). The more information that students have on a topic, the better inferences they will make. Students make inferences during and after the reading of nonfiction texts. To make an inference, students must make an educated guess and reach a conclusion that is based on the information presented in the text. Inferential thinking comes in handy when students need to find the answer to a question that is not directly answered in the text.

Students with strong reading skills are able to infer implicit information from the text and develop meaning based on that information. If students have weak inferential skills, they will not be able to understand the underlying meaning of the text they have just read.

Infer Meaning

Strategy 1: Reaction Journal

Recording their reactions to a text becomes a natural occurrence when students keep a reaction journal. For every piece of nonfiction text students read, have them record their reaction to the text. Always provide time for students to share their reactions either with a buddy, in a small group, or in a whole-class activity. (Standard 7.4)

Strategy 2: Interpreting the Author's Meaning

For this strategy, students work in groups to interpret the author's meaning. Read a piece of text to the class that students can use to interpret the author's meaning. Divide students into small groups to discuss the text. Students should discuss information that is implied but not directly stated. Using page 91, students write the inferences they make. Then they write two clues from the text that they used to make these inferences. Students also have the opportunity to write about any previous knowledge they used to help make these inferences. (Standards 5.2, 7.4, 8.2)

Strategy 3: Reactions to Nonfiction Text

Break up the class into small, heterogeneous, cooperative groups. Make sure each group has a competent reader, a competent writer, and someone who will keep the group on task. Also make sure that the group of students will work well together. Assign a job to each student in the group. There can be a **Relater** (the reader), a **Recorder** (the writer), a **Manager** (the task keeper), and a **Reporter** (someone who reports the group's reactions). Assign all groups the same nonfiction text to read. The Relater reads the article to the group. Then the group will discuss their reactions to the text. The Recorder writes all of the reactions on a copy of page 92. The Manager makes sure that all members state their reactions, watching the clock to allow everyone time to talk before time is up. Finally, when the groups reconvene, the Reporter will present the reactions to the class. Afterward, have a class discussion about the similarities and differences of the different groups' reactions. Remind the class to respect and value all the reactions of their classmates. (Standard 8.5)

Strategy 4: Prior Knowledge Inference

The teacher introduces this strategy by having students make inferences about body language and facial expressions. For example, the teacher shows students a face with a frown and has them infer that the person is unhappy. A picture of a person shrugging has them infer that the person is confused or indifferent. Teachers should emphasize to students that they were able to make these inferences because of their personal experiences related to emotions and body language. Students can identify their prior knowledge on a topic and what they think they will learn based on previewing. Model this strategy several times with students before having them try it. The teacher can choose a student to make a face and the teacher can practice inferring what the student is thinking. The student can confirm whether the teacher was correct. Once students feel comfortable with this activity, try giving students books to practice their inferring skills. After students read, they identify what they learned and engage in a discussion in which they connect new information to their prior knowledge and the information gained during previewing. (Standards 7.4, 8.5)

Infer Meaning

Strategy 5: Plot vs. Theme

Both nonfiction and fiction texts are full of themes. Usually, most nonfiction texts have one main idea but several themes for readers to think about and infer. When you are discussing the differences between plot and themes, it is important to use a familiar text to discuss plot. Plot usually occurs in a narrative or a fiction text. The plot is the series of actions that occur in a book. Themes represent the bigger ideas of the story. Themes are usually inferred and often make us feel emotions. Use the template on page 93 to discuss plot and themes. Begin with a familiar fiction text. Have students write the plot of the story. Discuss the theme or themes that are represented in the book. It is important for students to give the reasoning behind the theme or themes chosen. Next, read a nonfiction book. Chart the plot and theme(s) of this book. (Standards 5.2, 7.4, 8.2)

Strategy 6: Facts and Inferences

This strategy is very useful when you are reading textbooks. Start by discussing what facts and inferences are. Facts are things that we can see or observe. Inferences are interpretations we make before, during, or after reading. Use the Facts and Inferences template on page 94 to model this strategy. Begin by reading a short passage aloud to the class. Ask the class to tell what facts they heard in the passage. List the facts on the "facts" side of the paper. Next, go through and have students identify any interpretations that they can make based on the facts they know. Put these on the "inferences" side of the page. Continue until the class is comfortable with the process. Eventually, the class should be able to use this template alone or with a partner. (Standards 7.1, 7.2, 8.2)

Strategy 7: Questioning and Inferring

Questioning and inferring work together to build comprehension. When students are questioning what they are reading, they are trying to make connections. Model this strategy first with the whole class. Use the templates for questioning and inferring on pages 95 and 96. Read aloud a nonfiction text. Stop periodically to ask for any questions students may have. Put those questions on the "questions" side of the paper. Continue reading, writing any questions the students may have. Next, go back and write any inferences that students make. At the end, connect any questions and inferences that are similar. (Standard 8.2)

Strategy 8: Using Pictures for Inference

This strategy works well because using pictures to derive meaning is a very familiar strategy to most readers. When students use pictures to figure out a text, they are making inferences. This strategy can be used after the teacher has used similar strategies to teach inference. Begin by choosing a picture book and copying the activity on page 97 for each student in the class. Together, the class starts with the cover of the book. The teacher reads the title and has students look at the cover and explain what they see. For example, if the title is *The Horrible Day*, the teacher asks students why the day may be horrible and fills out the chart discussing the title and the illustrations on the cover. The class discusses why they chose the answer they did, with the teacher pointing out any inferences. As the teacher reads through the book, students discuss and list other pictures and inferences. (Standards 5.1, 5.2, 8.2)

Infer Meaning

Strategy 9: Infer with Pictures

The teacher chooses a picture from a piece of nonfiction text the class is reading, photocopies the picture, and copies it onto the activity on page 98. Students can make inferences using the picture and describe the information that is shown in the picture. Then students should think about what else the picture might be telling them that isn't shown exactly in the picture. The teacher explains that this is a type of inference. (Standards 5.1, 5.2, 7.4, 8.2)

Strategy 10: Making Predictions with the Title

Students can be taught to make predictions using the title of the text they are going to read. The activity on page 99 can be used for practice with this strategy. The teacher can guide students to think about the subject of the book based on the title and ask them what some of the words in the book might be. After reading the text, students can decide if they think the title of the book was a good choice. If not, they can suggest a better title for the book. (Standards 5.2, 8.2)

Strategy 11: Directed Reading-Thinking Activity (DRTA)

The directed reading-thinking activity (DRTA) actively involves students in the reading process. The students predict, read, and prove their predictions while the teacher asks questions such as:

"What do you think?"

"Why do you think that?"

"How can you prove your predictions?"

In the DRTA, students are asked to make predictions before reading a selected part of a text. Next they read until the determined stopping point of the pre-selected text. They then go back through the text to find evidence to support their predictions. Students with incorrect predictions are encouraged to find support. Proving or disproving a prediction involves the same process. Many times, this activity gives students permission to stretch their thinking. The focus is placed on the process of proving their predictions by using the text. Before beginning this strategy, the teacher must pre-read the text to determine stopping points. This decision can sometimes be challenging for the teacher. Start by slowing down your process of reading. Listen to your "inner reading voice" that asks questions or makes connections. When you come to a point in the reading that suggests a question or makes you wonder about something or helps you make a connection, this is a great place to stop and ask that question of the class. Use the DRTA template on page 100 with this strategy. (Standards 5.2, 5.7, 8.2)

Strategy 12: Direct Inquiry Activity (DIA)

The direct inquiry activity (DIA) uses the same process as the DRTA. The DIA is better for texts that include many facts and a lot of information. In the DIA, students use five key questions to make predictions. The questions are "Who," "What," "Where," "How," and "Why." Use the DIA template on page 101 for this strategy. (Standards 5.2, 8.2)

Infer Meaning

Strategy 13: Reciprocal Teaching Chart

Reciprocal teaching incorporates four basic skills that can be used with students of all ages and backgrounds. These skills can be used independently of each other, or all four of them can be used when discussing a text. The four skills of reciprocal teaching are outlined below:

1. **Questioning:** Students develop their own questions about what has just been read. These questions are answered by the other students and might require the use of inferential thinking.
2. **Summarizing:** Students retell the main points of the text using their own words.
3. **Clarifying:** Students share with the group or class what thought processes were used in clearing up confusing parts or ambiguity in the text.
4. **Predicting:** Students predict what they think will happen or what they think will be covered next in the text based on the information that has been read.

Using a reciprocal teaching method guides students to make inferences about the material they are reading. This strategy helps students think beyond the actual printed words on the page. For this strategy, the teacher places students in partners and gives them a short nonfiction piece to read together. After reading, the pairs summarize the text together. Then students should ask each other questions about the reading. Each partner can help the other clarify the text based on the questions asked. Finally, students can predict what they think will happen next. Using this method in a small-group or partner setting helps students develop these inferring skills. Copy the chart on page 102 for students to keep in their writing folders as a reference. Model this strategy several times until students are comfortable using it. Once students are comfortable with this strategy, the activity on page 103 can be used as a guide. (Standards 5.2, 7.3, 8.2, 8.5)

Strategy 14: Using Picture Books

Using picture books is a great place to start when teaching inferences. Wordless books help students build meaning as they look at the pictures. Practicing making inferences with a familiar genre such as fiction will help students transfer the skills to nonfiction.

Choose a picture book that has very few words or none at all. Go through the book with the class, eliciting a story from the group. After reading the story, have students respond to the book. Notice the details that students choose to put in their pictures. As a group, share what each student drew and wrote. Discuss with the class the details that they had to infer from the book. For example, ask "Why does your picture have someone smiling?" or "How did you know this person was happy?"

Extension: After you have practiced this strategy with a fiction text, read a nonfiction text to the class. You may want to choose a book that is about an animal or a subject that is familiar to students. Trade books are a great source for informational texts that are at students' diverse reading levels. (Standards 5.1, 5.2, 8.5)

Infer Meaning

Interpreting the Author's Meaning

Directions: Read the text that your teacher has given you. Discuss in a small group any information the author has not directly stated, but has implied. Write the inference you make. Then write two clues. Finally, write anything that you already knew that led you to infer the author's meaning.

Title: _____

Inference: _____

_____

Clues:

  1. _____

     _____

  2. _____

     _____

Previous knowledge: _____

_____

_____

_____

_____

Infer Meaning

Reactions to Nonfiction Text

Group Members

The Relater: _____   The Manager: _____

The Recorder: _____   The Reporter: _____

Directions: Listen closely as the Relater reads the text assigned by your teacher. The three other members of the group can jot down their reactions on scratch paper. When the Relater has finished reading, the Manager will call on members one at a time to give a reaction. The Manager will allow the Recorder time to write down each reaction before moving to the next member. Finally, the Reporter will report the reactions of the group to the whole class.

Title of the Text: _____

Reactions

Member 1: _____

_____

_____

Member 2: _____

_____

_____

Member 3: _____

_____

_____

Member 4: _____

_____

_____

Infer Meaning

Plot vs. Theme

Directions: First, write the title of the book. In the top left column, describe the plot of the book. In the top right column, write the theme(s). Then write your reaction and conclusion in the bottom two boxes.

Title: _____

Plot	Theme
Reaction	**Conclusion**

Infer Meaning

Facts and Inferences

Directions: Read the passage. List the facts from the passage in the left column. In the right column, across from each fact, write your understanding of that fact.

Facts	Inferences

Infer Meaning

Questioning and Inferring—Part 1

Directions: Listen to the passage as the teacher reads. Write the title of the text in the center circle. Write questions in the circles extending from the left of the center circle. Write inferences made based on these questions in the circles extending from the right of the center circle.

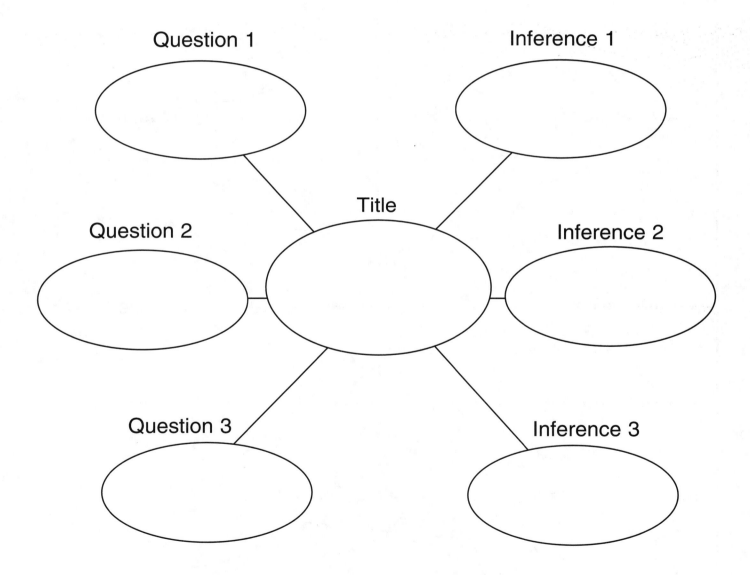

Question 1

Inference 1

Title

Question 2

Inference 2

Question 3

Inference 3

Infer Meaning

Questioning and Inferring—Part 2

Directions: Listen to the passage as the teacher reads. Write the title of the text in the center circle. Write questions in the circles extending from the center circle. Write inferences made based on these questions in the circles extending from the question circles.

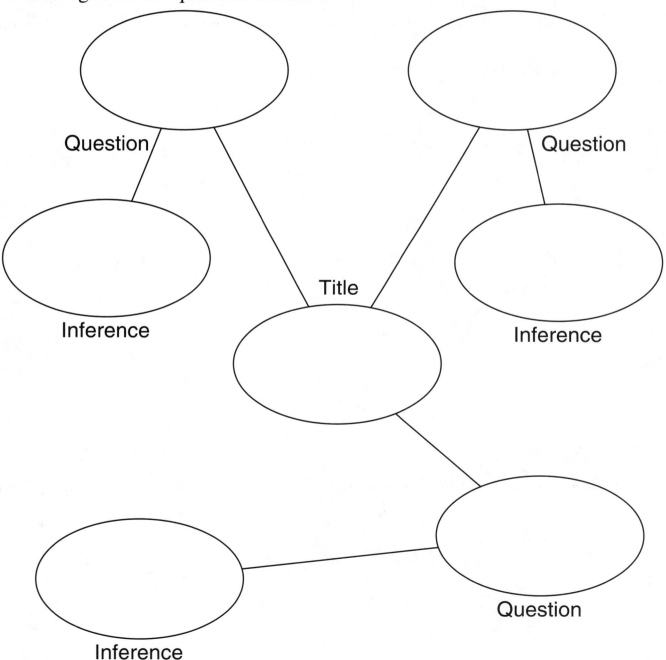

Question

Question

Inference

Title

Inference

Question

Inference

Infer Meaning

Using Pictures for Inference

Directions: From the picture book you are reading, record pictures or illustrations in the "Picture" column. In the "Inference" column, explain or interpret what you see.

Picture	Inference

Infer Meaning

Infer with Pictures

Directions: Look at the picture below. Read the directions under the picture.

Book title:_____

```



```

Write three sentences about the information shown in this picture.

1. _____

2. _____

3. _____

Write three sentences that can be inferred about this picture.

1. _____

2. _____

3. _____

© Shell Education

Infer Meaning

Making Predictions with the Title

Directions: Write the title of the book you are going to read. Then read the first two questions and answer them before reading. After reading, answer the third question.

Book title:_____

Before reading the text

1. What do you think this book will be about?

   _____

   _____

   _____

2. What are some of the words that might be used in this text?

   _____   _____   _____

   _____   _____   _____

   _____   _____   _____

After reading the text

3. Do you think the title of this book was a good choice? If not, what would be a better title for this book?

   _____

   _____

   _____

Infer Meaning

Directed Reading-Thinking Activity (DRTA)

Directions: As you read, stop to predict what will come next. Write your prediction in the left column. Then go back to the text to find support for your prediction. Write the evidence in the "Proof" section.

Predictions	Proof

Infer Meaning

Direct Inquiry Activity (DIA)

Directions: As you read, use the following chart to write your predictions.

? ? ? ? ? ?

Who?	
What?	
Where?	
How?	
Why?	

Infer Meaning

Reciprocal Teaching Chart

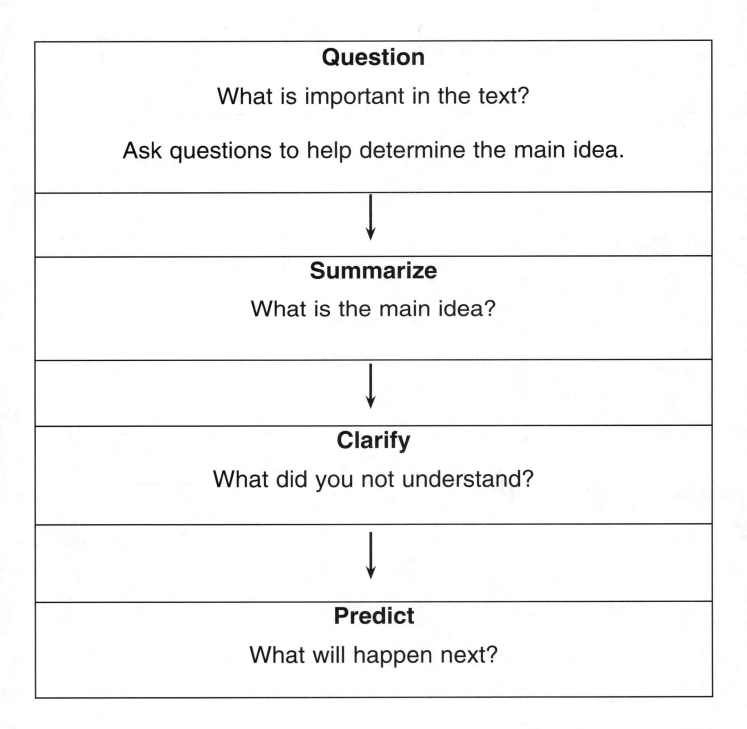

Question

What is important in the text?

Ask questions to help determine the main idea.

↓

Summarize

What is the main idea?

↓

Clarify

What did you not understand?

↓

Predict

What will happen next?

Infer Meaning

Reciprocal Teaching Guide

Directions: Use this activity as you read the selection.

Name: _____

Title of Selection: _____

Prediction: _____

_____

_____

Read.

Was the prediction right? (Yes or No) _____

Why? _____

_____

_____

Question: _____

_____

_____

Clarify: _____

_____

_____

Summarize: _____

_____

_____

Notes

Ask Questions

PASSPORT TO COMPREHENSION

Ask Questions

Asking questions is an important tool to use for grabbing students' attention and for motivating them to read nonfiction texts. Students who can ask and answer key questions are able to discuss the text effectively, relate the text to their lives and the world, and clarify and understand the information presented in the text (Harvey and Goudvis 2000).

Successful discussions centered on asking and answering questions about a text have many positive results. Students are able to share personal knowledge and background information about the topic and begin building a foundation for sharing and thinking about nonfiction texts (Rasinski and Padak 2000). Through class or group discussions, students are stimulated to develop and ask new questions about the topic or subject.

Types of Questions

Two categories of questions are **authentic questions** and **literal questions**. An authentic question is one that is asked because the person asking the question does not know the answer. Answers to authentic questions generally require students to use higher-level critical thinking skills instead of supplying a rote answer. An example of an authentic question is "What do you think about (topic) and why?" Students' development of authentic questions arises from their interest being whetted by a topic, causing students to ask questions in order to learn more about the topic. Students with a sincere, authentic question become motivated and set a purpose for wanting to read and learn more about the topic (Harvey 1998). A literal question is quite different from an authentic question. When the teacher (or student) asks a literal question, the answer is already known by the person doing the asking (Rasinski and Padak 2000). Literal questions are frequently asked after reading a story and require students to recall specific information when answering the question.

Promoting the Use of Questions

Primary-age students sometimes have difficulty forming questions. Quite often when the teacher asks, "Does anyone have a question about this topic?" students might answer, "Yes, I like it!" Primary-age students need to be taught how to ask and answer questions to suit a variety of purposes and learning activities. Harvey (1998) suggests incorporating questioning strategies across the curriculum by using different activities such as:

- holding small group or whole-class discussions
- reading aloud and sharing the thought processes used in asking a question
- having students identify and share those "burning" or "I wonder" questions they have about the topic
- playing different questioning games—such as 20 Questions or Animal, Vegetable, Mineral
- having a "question of the day" about a topic that is being studied
- mapping questions on a chart or story web
- reading newspapers or magazine articles that are of interest to students or relate to the topic being studied

Ask Questions

Promoting the Use of Questions *(cont.)*

Research shows that students' abilities to comprehend the information in nonfiction texts are greatly influenced by their own background knowledge, information, and experiences on the topic or subject matter (Anthony and Raphael 1996). Students who can read well know that asking questions increases their comprehension and understanding of the material presented in the nonfiction text (Keene and Zimmermann 1997).

Before introducing a text to students, the teacher surveys the text and develops questions on the key concepts that are covered in the text. When the teacher asks a question, he or she is modeling how to use questioning strategies to guide learning before, during, and after reading the text.

These questioning strategies are especially important for English language learners who may not be familiar with the words and phrases used in the text. Through questioning and different reading activities, second language learners are able to develop a foundation of background knowledge and then use this knowledge when reading nonfiction texts.

There are many types of questions that students or teachers might ask before, during, or after reading a nonfiction text. According to Harvey (1998), Harvey and Goudvis (2000), and Fountas and Pinnell (2001), some of the different kinds of questions that can be asked are:

- questions that can be answered by locating the information in the text
- questions that are asked to clarify confusing and ambiguous statements
- questions that can be answered by making inferences based on the information presented in the text
- questions that require the recalling of specific information
- questions that prompt some type of emotional response
- questions that summarize the information
- questions that promote the synthesizing of information
- questions that can be answered through one's own background knowledge and prior experiences
- questions that construct meaning and enhance understanding
- questions to discover new information or ideas
- questions that require further research
- questions that develop and expand students' background knowledge

Through the use of questions, students are able to see the connections between the text and the real world. Asking questions also helps students visualize the information, make inferences and predictions based on the known information, synthesize the information, and identify the relevant facts covered in the text (Harvey and Goudvis 2000).

Students with strong reading and comprehension skills are active participants in the educational process. Research shows that students with good comprehension skills will know how to identify cue words that signal when important information is being presented in the text and will be able to group these pieces of information together to see the "big picture."

Ask Questions

Promoting the Use of Questions *(cont.)*

Students who develop questions during the reading of nonfiction texts are beginning to anticipate what will come next in the text. By "thinking ahead," students are able to look for information that will prove or disprove their predictions (Anthony and Raphael 1996; Harvey 1998). Self-questioning strategies that are used while reading texts serve many vital functions. According to Harvey (1998), Anthony and Raphael (1996), and Robb (2000), self-questioning strategies:

- make students aware of any comprehension problems
- encourage students to use different reading strategies to repair any faulty misconceptions
- serve to improve students' comprehension of the material being read
- aid students in setting a purpose for reading
- motivate students to read in order to discover the answers to their questions
- make students aware of what they already know about a topic
- make students aware of what they need to learn about a topic
- increase students' knowledge base on a topic
- clarify any confusing statements
- enable students to monitor their comprehension and understanding of the information
- enable students to adjust or change reading strategies to make the information understandable and comprehensible

Before Reading Questions

The goals for any prereading strategy are:

- to activate students' prior knowledge, information, and experiences that relate to the topic
- to build a foundation for learning the new information
- to focus students' attention on the relevant facts and details
- to set a purpose for reading
- to have students share any questions they may have about the topic before reading the text
- to have students express background knowledge or information that may be inaccurate or is irrelevant to the topic being studied

---

Example of Inaccurate Information

In baseball, there are different positions on the team. One of the positions is the pitcher. The pitcher throws the ball to the batter.

This is what the text is describing.   This is what the student understands.

Ask Questions

Asking Open-Ended Questions

Asking questions is a core element in using nonfiction text for promoting further research into a given subject and for encouraging the sharing of diverse opinions and perspectives. Open-ended questions require students to think critically about the information in the text (Fountas and Pinnell 2001). Open-ended questions may have more than one correct answer as long as that particular answer can be supported with facts, information, and details from the text. Some open-ended questions might ask for students' opinions, but students still need to support their opinions with facts and details from the text.

Robb (2000) has compiled a list of open-ended questions that can be adjusted to fit just about any nofiction text:

- How does the title connect to the nonfiction text?
- Why did you select this subject to study?
- What new, unusual, or interesting facts did you learn?
- After reading the text, are there any other questions that you would like to ask and learn more about?
- After reading the text, have you changed your mind or opinion about the topic? Why or why not?

The teacher can easily expand upon or adjust the open-ended questions listed above by incorporating questions that use specific verbs. Robb (2000) has compiled a list of verbs frequently used when asking open-ended questions.

Verbs Used to Ask Open-Ended Questions					
analyze	ask why	classify	compare	connect	contrast
design	evaluate	examine	relate	show	

Research shows that students' knowledge of text structures and comprehension-monitoring techniques have a direct impact on their understanding of the nonfiction text (Anthony and Raphael 1996). Students who have an understanding of text organization and monitoring strategies will have an easier time reading, understanding, and recalling the information presented in the text (Anthony and Raphael 1996).

The types of questions the teacher asks can enhance students' abilities to recall recently learned information and can promote their understandings of information in the content areas (Anthony and Raphael 1996). When planning lessons, the teacher surveys the text to identify the key concepts and develops questions that focus on these concepts. The teacher models a variety of questioning strategies that allow students to:

- recognize the important facts and details
- access their prior knowledge and information on the topic
- develop an awareness of the different text structures
- integrate this new knowledge with their prior knowledge on the topic (Anthony and Raphael 1995)

Ask Questions

Thought-Provoking Questions and Clarification Questions

Questions open the doors to further learning and increased understanding (Harvey and Goudvis 2000). By asking questions, students' curiosity increases and they are motivated to find out the answers to their questions. This motivation is the basis for research and takes students deeper into the nonfiction text.

Authentic questions are questions whose answers are unknown to both the teacher and the students. These questions often contain issues that students wonder about, and thus require further research on the part of the students. When students have authentic questions about a text, they are more likely to become engrossed in the text and become motivated to find out more about the topic.

Primary-age students are naturally curious about everyone and everything around them. By asking questions, students are able to make discoveries about the world around them, target their attention on the more important facts and details, and ask questions on a higher level (Keene and Zimmermann 1997). Students who are able to ask questions are able to set the purpose for reading, for further research, and for personally interacting with the information in the nonfiction text (Robb 2000). When reading nonfiction texts, students raise new questions as they read new information and connect the information to what is already known about the subject (Robb 2000). Students with strong reading skills continually ask questions before, during, and after reading the text. Students ask questions to:

- clarify ambiguous statements
- predict what will happen next in the text
- figure out the author's meaning, intent, style, and text structure
- locate information that answers a specific question (Keene and Zimmermann 1997)

The teacher needs to model the thinking processes used in asking questions and provide support and prompting to students when they are asking questions.

Strategy 1: Shared Questioning

Shared questioning has been shown to be particularly effective in helping challenged readers construct meaning in nonfiction texts since the shared teaching and learning approach tends to sustain their interest and keep them focused. Pair students, then follow these steps:

1. Both partners read the first paragraph silently and confer to decide the answer to a critical thinking question that you have posed.

2. One of the pair then writes the answer.

3. Partner A reads the second paragraph quietly to Partner B, who listens to come up with an answer to a question Partner A will ask.

4. Partner B reads the third paragraph quietly to Partner A, who listens to come up with an answer to a question Partner B will pose.

5. Both partners read the rest of the passage silently and confer to design an answer to a question you pose at the end of class. The answer to this question will be written independently by each student for homework. (Standards 5.2, 8.2)

Ask Questions

Strategy 2: Think Before Reading

The think-before-reading activity activates students' prior knowledge of a topic, has students generate questions about that topic, and focuses students' attention on finding the information that will answer specific questions (Anthony and Raphael 1996).

The think-before-reading activity is a three-step process:

1. Students write the topic or subject matter that the nonfiction text covers on the activity sheet.
2. Students write several sentences listing the things they would like to learn more about in regard to the topic.
3. Students generate questions about the topic.

Think Before Reading

Title: *Nursing*

My book is about: Nursing

Three things I would like to know are:

1. Why do nurses give people shots?
2. How long does it take to become a nurse?
3. Are nurses the same as doctors?

Questions that I have are:

1. Why do nurses wear white?
2. Are there different kinds of nurses?
3. Do nurses get sick?

The think-before-reading activity can easily be done with the whole class or with a small group of students. Students can dictate their responses, and the teacher can record the responses on a large sheet of chart paper or on a transparency. Use the template on page 118 for practice with this strategy. (Standards 7.4, 8.2)

Strategy 3: Organizational Guides—Question Guide

Organizational guides enable students to organize information, identify key words and phrases, and locate the important facts and details covered in the text. Organizational guides show students how the information is organized in the text. This guide can enhance students' abilities to understand and recall information in the nonfiction text (Anthony and Raphael 1996). There are many types of organizational guides (graphic organizers) that can be used with different types of nonfiction text structures. Some examples are story maps, idea maps, and pattern guides.

Use the organizational guide on page 119 (Question Guide), to teach this strategy. Model how to use this strategy several times before having students try it independently. (Standards 5.2, 5.6, 7.1, 7.2)

Ask Questions

Strategy 4: Content and Process Questions—Ask Me!

According to Anthony and Raphael (1996), questions asked before and during the reading of the text should center on content questions and process questions. Content questions are used to check students' understandings of the text and are connected to the purpose for reading the text. Content questions are questions that can be answered by using the information presented in the text and are asked after students have read a specific portion of the text.

Process questions focus on the reading strategies that students use to arrive at a specific meaning. According to Anthony and Raphael (1996), specific process questions have students:

- make predictions
- prove or disprove predictions
- identify elements of the text that signal important ideas, such as using bold print, italic print, underlining words in paragraphs, etc.

The following are examples of process questions:

- What questions did you develop after reading the title of the text?
- What information in the text did you use in making the prediction?
- What new or confusing words did you come across when reading the text?
- How could you figure out the meaning of a new or unfamiliar word?
- What is the main idea of the text? What in the text made you think that was the main idea?
- Did the author do a good job of writing the text? Why or why not?

These are the kinds of questions students need to ask in order to monitor their own level of comprehension and understanding of the text (Anthony and Raphael 1996). It is important that the teacher asks students questions during the reading process to set them on the right path to becoming independent and strategic readers and thinkers. The template on page 120 can be used when teaching this strategy. (Standards 5.2, 5.7, 7.2, 8.2)

Strategy 5: Asking All the Right Questions

As students read, they need to keep the 5 Ws (who, what, when, where, and why) in mind at all times. Help them with this task by distributing a copy of the Asking All the Right Questions graphic organizer on page 121 and having them fill it in as they read. (Standard 8.2)

Who? American colonists

When? July 4, 1776

Why? wanted their own government and laws

What? said they were independent from England

Where? Philadelphia, Pennsylvania

Ask Questions

Strategy 6: Asking the 5 Ws and H Questions

Before reading the nonfiction text, the teacher demonstrates how to ask questions and generate predictions that answer the 5 Ws and H questions (who, what, where, when, why, and how) (Tarasoff 1993). The teacher will model asking literal questions as well as inferential questions. It is important that students be asked some inferential questions that require them to interpret the information in the nonfiction text, as well as connect it to their background knowledge on the subject (Anthony and Raphael 1996).

For example, when learning about tigers, the following questions might be generated:

- Why do tigers have long tails? (literal)
- What are tigers' natural enemies? (literal or inferential)
- What animals do tigers hunt? (literal)
- Where do tigers live? (literal)
- When do tigers hunt? (literal)
- How do tigers escape from danger? (literal)
- Looking at a tiger's teeth, what kind of food do you think the tiger likes to eat? (inferential)
- How do the tiger's stripes help him survive? (inferential)

After modeling how to ask different types of questions, the teacher can have students generate questions on topics that are of interest to them. To help support students in asking questions, the teacher can write the 5 Ws and H on the board or on a large piece of chart paper for students to use when developing questions on the topic. The teacher can also use the activity on page 122. (Standard 8.2)

Strategy 7: Ask the Writer

With the ask-the-writer strategy, students engage in an independent dialogue with the text. They write questions as they think of them, then decide whether they were answered in the text. When the questions are answered by the text, students record the page number of the answer and a brief explanation. For each question the text did not answer, students write plans for finding the answer in the "Tell more" column.

Questions you have for the writer	Answered?	Tell more . . .
1. What is a mammal?	No (Yes) ⟶ p. 156 a warm-blooded animal with fur or hair that gives milk to its young	
2. Are monkeys mammals?	No (Yes) ⟶ p. 157	
3. Do all mammals sweat?	(No) Yes ⟶ p.	ask teacher

Use the activity on page 123 for practice with this strategy. (Standard 8.2)

Ask Questions

Strategy 8: Concept Attainment

With concept attainment (Schwartz and Raphael 1985), students organize conceptual information by analyzing different attributes in response to five questioning prompts.

1. Preview the material, select a key concept, and initiate a discussion.

2. Ask students to brainstorm information that could answer each of the five questions that are listed in the sample chart below. List the information on the concept-attainment chart. Brainstorming is crucial, since listening to the associations and explanations of others helps students add to their own knowledge base. It also empowers academically weak students by letting them know that they already have some knowledge of the topic to be studied. In addition, it helps you determine students' levels of prior knowledge about the subject.

3. Summarize the knowledge that has been shared through the brainstorming, being certain to correct inaccurate information.

4. Leave the class chart up and ask students to select information from it to fill in their own Concept Attainment graphic organizer (see page 124). This activity enables students to pick the information that they find most comprehensible or memorable. (In the chart below, under "electricity," one student may have chosen to compare electricity to trees because both are jeopardized by lightning.) (Standards 5.2, 7.3, 7.4, 8.2)

To introduce the concept-attainment chart, give some simple, concrete examples such as:

What is it?	What is it like?	How are they alike?	What is its category?	What is another example?
electricity	lumber	both renewable resources	natural resource	gas
grizzly bear	wolf	both eat other animals	mammal	polar bear
apple	peach	both round foods with a peel	fruit	orange

Strategy 9: Knowledge Tier

Prior to reading a passage with the class, read through a nonfiction passage and design a knowledge tier. This technique will help students recognize the important questions and concentrate on the most essential components. A knowledge tier has three levels. For the base, choose three to five important concepts that students should remember and build on throughout their lives. This is core knowledge that all literate adults know. For the middle, choose three to five concepts that will be useful knowledge, things that may be forgotten after the unit, but that the student may be able to recall years later in response to a stimulus. At the top, put three to five details that will definitely be forgotten after the unit is over. These are the things that most literate adults do not know (although they would probably know how to locate the information). Display the knowledge tier and guide your class to turn the items you've listed in the bottom two levels into questions. A blank template is on page 125. (Standard 8.2)

Ask Questions

Strategy 9: Knowledge Tier *(cont.)*

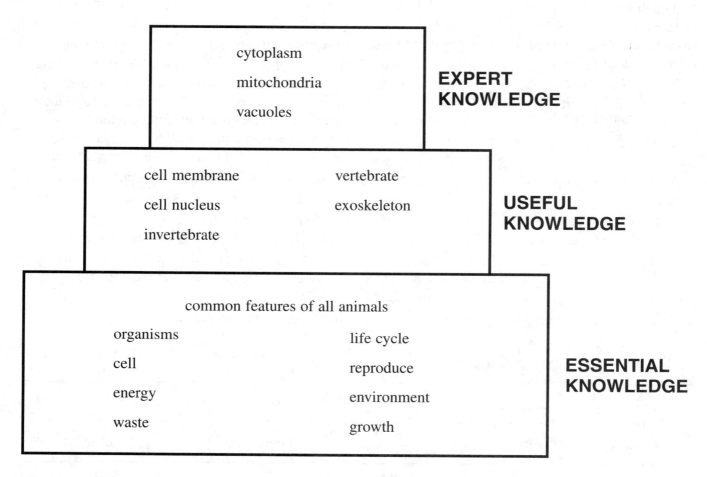

Class-generated questions:

What are the common features of all animals?

What are organisms?

How does energy relate to animals?

What is waste?

What is a life cycle?

What does it mean to reproduce?

What is an environment and what does it have to do with animals?

What are a cell membrane and a cell nucleus?

What is the difference between an invertebrate and a vertebrate?

What is an exoskeleton?

STRATEGIES
AND
SKILLS

Ask Questions

Strategy 10: Why? Pie

You can use the Why? Pie strategy to help students identify essential relationships between objects or concepts. Using the template on page 126, model the strategy by having students read an expository passage and then ask questions that begin with the word *why* and can only be answered by making inferences (the answer is not directly stated in the article). Then have students read further and work in pairs to come up with *why* questions about the material and to discuss possible responses to their questions. Then they can exchange questions with another pair and develop responses to those questions as well. (Standards 7.1, 8.2) Here's an example of a student's Why? Pie after reading this article:

Floods happen when too much water runs into a stream or river. The stream or river gets so high it goes right over its banks. Floods drown people and animals. Floods can wash away houses, cars, and bridges. They hurt crops and carry away topsoil. For thousands of years, people have tried to stop floods.

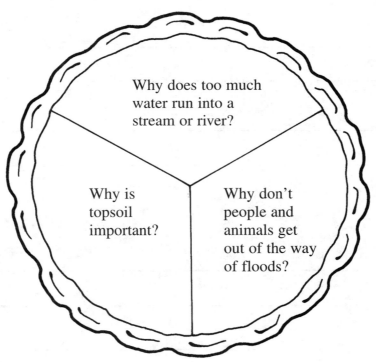

Why does too much water run into a stream or river?

Why is topsoil important?

Why don't people and animals get out of the way of floods?

Strategy 11: Question Web

A question web has a single, fundamental question written prominently in the center of a wheel (Harvey and Goudvis 2000). As students read the text, they add lines like spokes from the question hub. On these lines they write information that relates to the question. At the bottom of the sheet, students use the bits of information they've written on these lines to construct a one- or two-line answer to the question. Question webs are especially practical for small, cooperative research groups. The Question Web template is on page 127. (Standards 8.2, 8.5)

Ask Questions

Think Before Reading

Title: _____

My book is about: _____

Three things I would like to know:

1. _____

_____

2. _____

_____

3. _____

_____

Questions that I have:

1. _____

_____

2. _____

_____

3. _____

_____

Ask Questions

Organizational Guides—Question Guide

Directions: Choose a nonfiction book to read. While you read, think of questions you have about the book. Stop and write those questions below. Write the page number where you stopped to ask a question. After you finish reading, go back and see if you can answer your questions.

1. page _____

    My question: _____

    _____

2. page _____

    My question: _____

    _____

3. page _____

    My question: _____

    _____

4. page _____

    My question: _____

    _____

5. page _____

    My question: _____

    _____

6. page _____

    My question: _____

    _____

Ask Questions

Content and Process Questions—Ask Me!

Directions: Answer the following questions about your nonfiction book.

Before Reading

Read the title. What questions do you have about the book from reading the title?

1. What do you think this book will be about?

   _____

   _____

2. Why do you think so?

   _____

   _____

After Reading

3. What new or confusing words did you find in the book?

   _____

   _____

4. How could you find out the meanings of these words?

   _____

   _____

5. What is the main idea of the book?

   _____

   _____

6. What made you think so?

   _____

   _____

Ask Questions

Asking All the Right Questions

Directions: As you read the selection, answer the Who, What, When, Where, and Why questions. Write your answers in the ovals for each question.

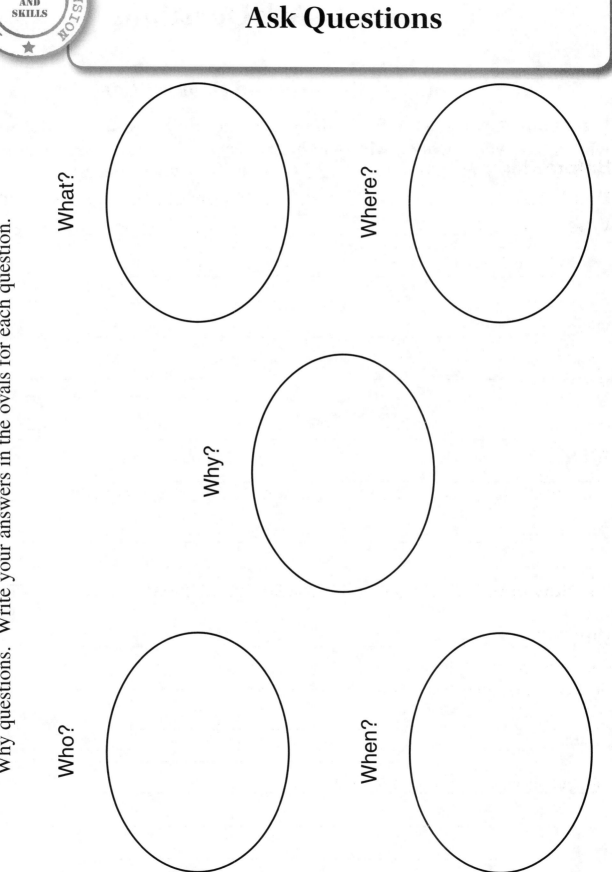

What?

Where?

Why?

Who?

When?

Ask Questions

Asking the 5 Ws and H Questions

Directions: Choose a nonfiction book to read. Before you read, think of a who, what, when, where, why, and how question that you have about the book below. After you read, go back and try to answer your questions.

Who? _____

_____

What? _____

_____

When? _____

_____

Where? _____

_____

Why? _____

_____

How? _____

_____

Ask Questions

Ask the Writer

Directions: As you read, write questions you have for the writer. Then decide whether the questions were answered in the text. Circle **No** or **Yes**. If the answer is **Yes**, write the page number where the answer can be found. You can write more information about the answer in the "Tell more" column. If the answer is **No**, write a plan for finding the answer in the "Tell more" column.

Questions you have for the writer	Answered?	Tell more . . .
1.	No Yes ⟶ p. _____	
2.	No Yes ⟶ p. _____	
3.	No Yes ⟶ p. _____	

Ask Questions

Concept Attainment

Directions: Fill out the chart below by answering all the questions.

What is it?	What is it like?	How are they alike?	What is its category?	What is another example?

Ask Questions

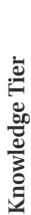

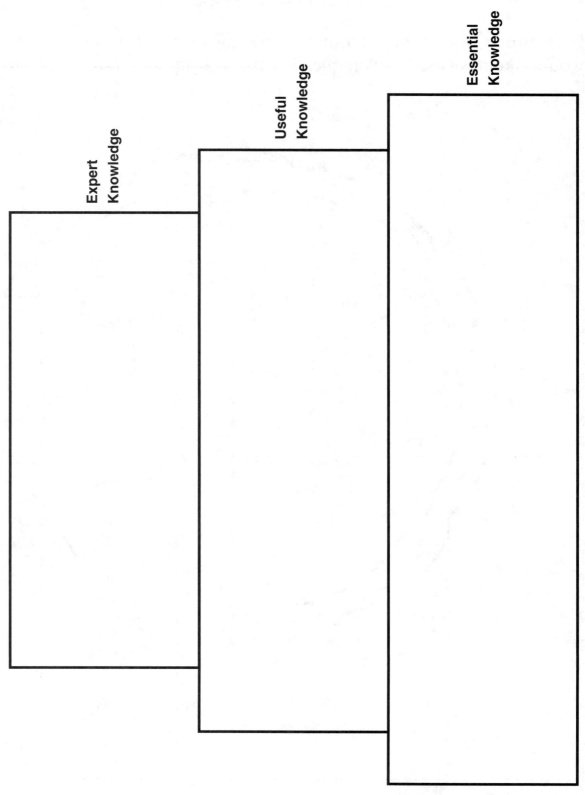

Essential Knowledge

Useful Knowledge

Expert Knowledge

Ask Questions

Why? Pie

Directions: In each pie section, write a question about what you read that you would like answered. Each question must begin with the word *Why*.

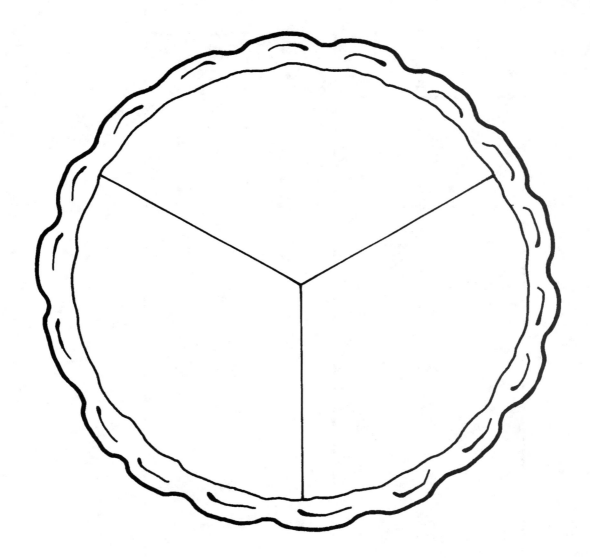

Ask Questions

Question Web

Directions: In the circle, write one important question about what you read. On the lines coming out of the circle, write information that relates to the question. Then write a one- to two-line answer to the question at the bottom of the page.

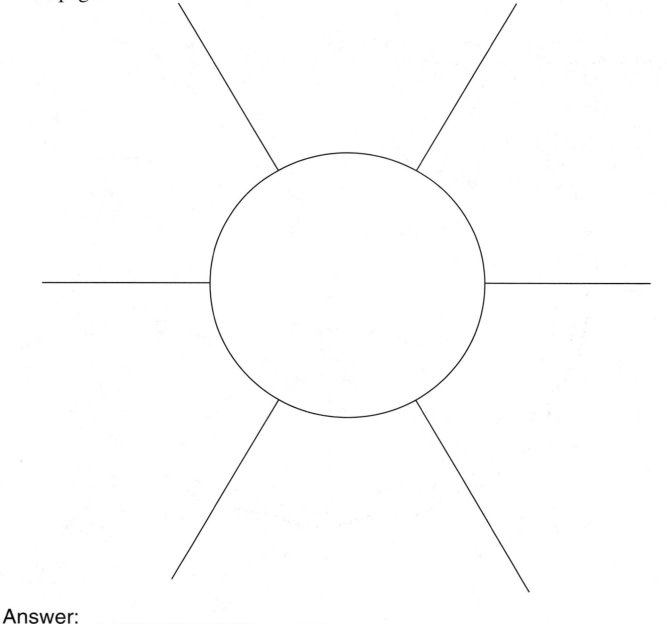

Answer: _____

_____

Notes

PASSPORT TO COMPREHENSION

Determine Importance

Determine Importance—
Main Idea and Supporting Details

Reading and comprehending nonfiction books in the early primary grades are often difficult for many students. Young students are accustomed to reading narrative stories and books that generally use patterned and predictable text. Students are often asked to tell about the beginning, middle, and ending of the story. Nonfiction text is written differently. Often it is not predictable or repetitive, and the information is written at a higher reading level than fiction. The text may contain many new concepts and unfamiliar vocabulary. When reading informational (expository) texts, students are asked to identify main ideas to show comprehension. Determining what is important in the text is crucial to comprehension.

Students need strategy instruction that teaches them how to locate the main idea in nonfiction passages and how to retell the important facts and details of expository text and graphic sources.

Strategy 1: Text Structure

Set students up for success by teaching them that many nonfiction texts have clues to help them find the main idea. Often, the main idea will be at the beginning or end of the passage or will contain bold print. Find examples of text or books that use these clues and train students to find the main idea in the first or last sections of the text. Also, teach them to read the bold print and the print around it to find the main idea. You want students to practice this strategy, but you also need to inform them that not all nonfiction texts use this pattern. It is a good place to start because it is predictable and students will be successful. Many students who did not know what a main idea was now have had some exposure and may be able to find it in other books with less obvious structures. (Standards 5.2, 7.1, 7.2, 7.4)

Strategy 2: Picture/Text Walk

Take students on a picture or text walk of the book or passage before you begin reading. As you go through the book page by page, stop to ask questions about the pictures and the text that force students to focus on the main idea. A picture or text walk can bring out key phrases and concepts while allowing students to link their own experiences with the main idea of the book prior to reading.

After students are familiar with using the text walk to begin identifying main ideas prior to reading, add another step. Teach students to ask questions that may be answered in their reading. The teacher should model this process in front of the class. "By reading this book, I think I am going to find the answer to the question _____. As I read, I am going to ask myself if I found the answer to my question." Begin by writing your question(s) and jotting down notes or a page number when you find the answer. Encourage students to write their questions prior to reading so that they will remember them or refer to them as they read. The teacher should ask questions about the main idea of the text. Modeling these questions shows students the kinds of questions they should ask themselves. Their questions may not always be about the main idea, but that is fine. By asking questions prior to reading and trying to answer them during reading, students will be actively engaged in the reading process. (Standards 5.1, 5.2, 7.1, 7.2)

Determine Importance—
Main Idea and Supporting Details

Strategy 3: Making Predictions

Making predictions before reading a book is another strategy that can be used to help students focus on the main idea in the book. The teacher may show the cover of the book and/or read the first page or two of the text and then stop to ask, "What do you think you will learn about in this book?" As students give their responses, they are asked to explain the reasons for their answers. These predictions may be written on a chart for discussion after the book has been read. By having students make predictions, the teacher is having them set their own purposes for reading. Making predictions will engage their attention and enhance comprehension. Use the activity on page 137 for practice with making predictions. (Standards 5.2, 7.2, 8.2)

Strategy 4: KWL Graphic Organizer

Donna Ogle developed the KWL teaching model, a strategy used to help readers focus on the main ideas in a text by accessing their prior knowledge. It works well with expository text. The letters stand for What I Know (K), What I Want to Know (W), and What I Learned (L). The steps in using a KWL chart are as follows:

1. **What I Know (K):** Students brainstorm what they know about a topic that they will be studying. The teacher records their responses under the K section of the chart. All responses are recorded, even those that may be incorrect. This section will be discussed after the book is read.

2. **What I Want to Know (W):** After students have shared the information that they already know, the teacher asks them what they would like to know about the topic. These responses are recorded in the W section. Students can refer to these as the book is being read.

3. **What I Learned (L):** This section is filled in after the book is read. Answers to the questions in the W section are recorded here, along with any new information learned in the book.

It is important for the teacher to review the chart with students after it is completed. As students share information, pose questions, and answer questions, they are actively involved in building their knowledge.

In the early grades, the KWL chart can be used for the whole group, with the teacher recording responses on a large class chart, the board, or a transparency. As students become familiar with the form and have practiced it with teacher guidance, they can begin to complete their KWL charts with a partner or individually with nonfiction books that may be available in the classroom during literacy centers. The KWL graphic organizer on page 138 can be used for practice. (Standards 7.4, 8.2, 8.5)

Determine Importance— Main Idea and Supporting Details

Strategy 5: Semantic Mapping

Semantic mapping is a strategy that can help students organize the information they know about a subject into different categories (Pearson and Johnson 1978). It is a visual representation of the subject. The steps for creating a semantic map are the following:

1. The subject being discussed is written on the board, a chart, or on a transparency. An oval is drawn around it.

2. Students think of words to describe the subject. As they share them, the teacher writes them on the chart in boxes and connects them to the oval with arrows. Above the arrows the teacher writes phrases or words to show the relationship between the subject and the other words.

3. Students give examples of the subject, and the teacher writes these in the ovals with arrows connecting them to the subject in the center oval.

The following is an example of a semantic map for insects:

Semantic Map for Insects

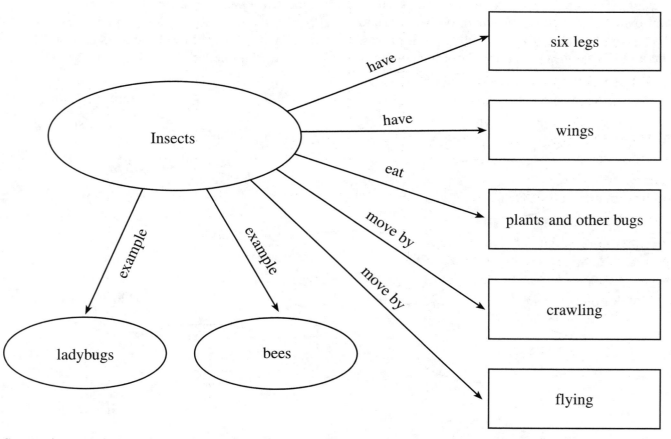

Semantic mapping is a strategy that works well when several books about the same subject are going to be read. As new information is learned, it can be added to the map. A blank graphic organizer is provided on page 139. (Standards 5.1, 7.1, 7.4, 8.2)

Determine Importance—Main Idea and Supporting Details

Strategy 6: Creative Mapping

Creative mapping combines semantic mapping with pictures (Naughton 1993). In this strategy a picture that represents the main idea is drawn. Then details that support the main idea are added around the picture. Creative mapping with drawings is an excellent graphic organizer to use with young students as they begin to explore nonfiction texts. The graphic organizers on pages 140 and 141 can be used for this strategy. (Standards 5.1, 7.1, 7.2, 7.4)

Strategy 7: Main Idea Web

Webs can be used before and after reading. In teaching students to find the main idea in nonfiction texts, using a web is an excellent strategy to use after the book has been read. In webs, the subject of the book is written in an oval on the board. Lines from the center oval are drawn to smaller ovals that relate to the subject in the center oval. Lines are then drawn from each smaller oval to the information students will share after the book is read. The template for a main idea web on page 142 can be used for this strategy. (Standards 5.1, 5.2, 7.1, 7.2, 7.3, 7.4)

For example, if students are going to read about penguins, the word *penguin* would be written in the center oval. Lines would be drawn out from it and attached to smaller ovals labeled "how it looks," "what it eats," "where it lives," and "how it moves." The information shared by students is then written at the end of the lines extending from the smaller ovals. See the example below.

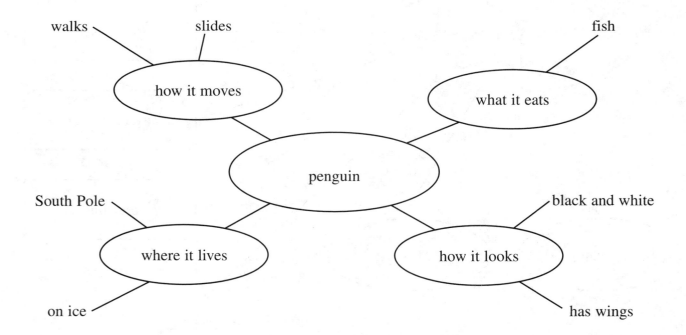

Determine Importance—
Main Idea and Supporting Details

Strategy 8: Understanding the Main Idea

This is another graphic organizer to use after reading. Students should write the main idea in the large box and draw a picture of it. Then, in the surrounding boxes, students write supporting details and draw pictures of each. Use the blank template on page 143 for this strategy. Alternative layouts are also included on pages 144 and 145. (Standards 5.1, 7.1, 7.2)

Strategy 9: Think-Aloud Chart

In using the think-aloud strategy, the teacher reads aloud to students, stopping at ends of sentences and other natural stopping places to talk about what he or she is thinking. Predicting, questioning, rereading, and using the text to figure out unfamiliar words are strategies to use during the think-aloud. The teacher's thoughts might include the following: "I wonder if . . .," "I think I know . . .," "I think we will learn . . .," and "In the picture I notice . . . ." Students should be listening only, not joining in as the teacher thinks aloud. The teacher should somehow signal the difference between reading and thinking aloud—perhaps by changing his or her voice, looking up, etc. After modeling the thinking, the teacher should make a chart of the thinking process as a visual for students as they discuss what they learned. It is important that the teacher has already read the book and has planned what he or she will say during the think-aloud. The teacher should continue the think-aloud strategy throughout the year. As students get more comfortable with it, the teacher can encourage and guide small groups to think aloud as they read new books. The Think-Aloud Chart on page 146 can be helpful when using this strategy. (Standards 5.1, 5.2, 5.4, 7.1, 7.2, 8.2)

Strategy 10: Sticky-Note Reading

This strategy can be used along with the think-aloud. While reading the selected book, the teacher can use sticky notes to keep track of his or her thinking. At a place where something is questioned or confusing, a question mark can be put on the sticky note and left on the appropriate page. These notes are useful when the students and teacher are creating a chart after the book has been read. They help students remember what is important in the book. After students have seen this procedure modeled many times, they can practice it themselves in groups or pairs during guided reading. (Standards 5.1, 7.2, 7.4, 8.2)

Strategy 11: Mini-Lesson: Finding the Main Idea

In this strategy, the teacher should write a short nonfiction paragraph before class begins rather than together with students. After the paragraph has been read once, the teacher should tell students that they will be looking for the main idea or supporting details, depending on which skill is being focused on in the lesson. The three activities on pages 147–149 provide practice in finding the main idea. Students should read each paragraph and underline the main idea. Students can work in small groups, pairs, or individually to complete this activity. (Standards 5.2, 7.1, 7.2)

Determine Importance— Main Idea and Supporting Details

Strategy 12: T-Chart

Reteach the strategy of finding the main idea and supporting details by using a T-chart. Put a T-chart on the board and ask students to think about the main idea and decide how to label the chart. Then ask them to think about the details from their reading and tell you which details go with which part of the main idea. When students feel comfortable with this strategy, have them fill out the T-Chart provided on page 150. (Standards 5.1, 5.2, 7.1, 7.2, 8.2)

For instance, you are teaching a geography lesson with the following main idea: There are many types of landforms and bodies of water. The T-chart below is an example for this lesson:

Main Idea: landforms	**Main Idea:** bodies of water
Examples: mountain, valley	**Examples:** lake, ocean
Details: size of mountain range or valley	**Details:** freshwater or saltwater

Strategy 13: Write Your Own Caption

Captions under photos or in the margins often contain the main idea or important information needed for comprehension of the text. Many students will skip these when reading independently. One activity that teaches students to read captions begins by showing them examples of texts with pictures and captions. Have them read the captions or you can read them aloud if they are too difficult. Next, have students use photos brought from home that do not need to be returned, or perhaps a cut-out magazine picture. Have them glue their pictures onto a piece of paper and then write captions for them. Compile these in a class book and let everyone practice reading captions. (Standards 5.1, 5.2, 7.4)

Strategy 14: Tables, Graphs, and Charts

Students need to be taught that important information in nonfiction texts often comes from graphics. Charts, tables, and graphs often contain the main idea or important information needed for comprehension of the text. Help students identify the main idea in graphic sources by giving them a variety of tables, graphs, and charts. Use direct instruction to show them what information is important and how to find information that the graphic is trying to communicate. (Standards 5.1, 5.2, 7.1, 7.2)

Determine Importance—
Main Idea and Supporting Details

Making Predictions

Directions: Answer the following questions in the spaces provided. What do you think the book will be about? What did you learn from reading the book? Then draw a picture of what you learned.

Book title: _____

I predict _____

_____

I learned _____

_____

Determine Importance—
Main Idea and Supporting Details

KWL Graphic Organizer

Directions: Write the title of the book you are going to read. Fill in the K and W sections before you read the book. Complete the L section after you have read the book.

Book title: _____

K: What I know	W: What I want to know	L: What I learned

#50468 Successful Strategies   © Shell Education

Determine Importance—
Main Idea and Supporting Details

Semantic Mapping

Directions: Fill in the map. Choose a topic. Think of examples for your topic. Then write words to describe your topic.

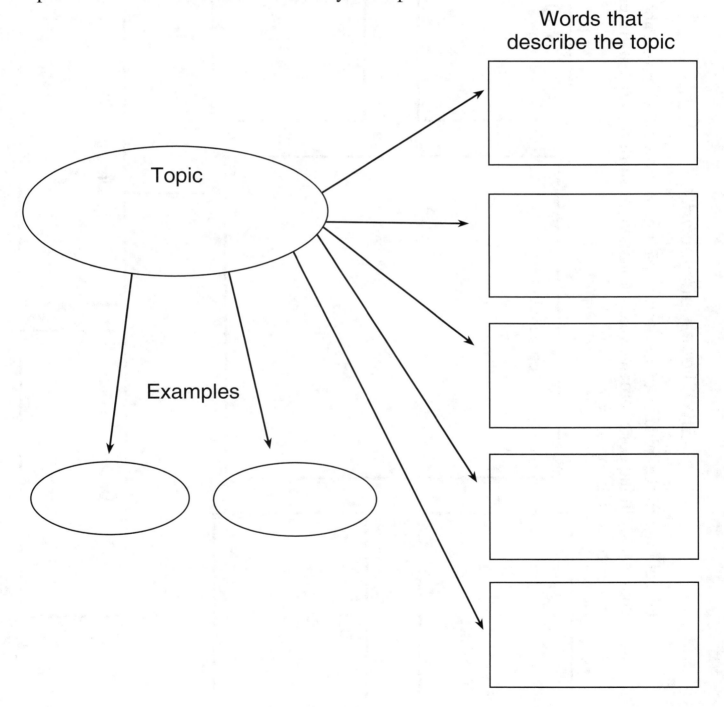

Words that describe the topic

Topic

Examples

Creative Mapping—Part 1

Directions: In the middle square, draw a picture of the topic you read about in your book. In the boxes around your picture, write words or draw pictures that tell more about your topic.

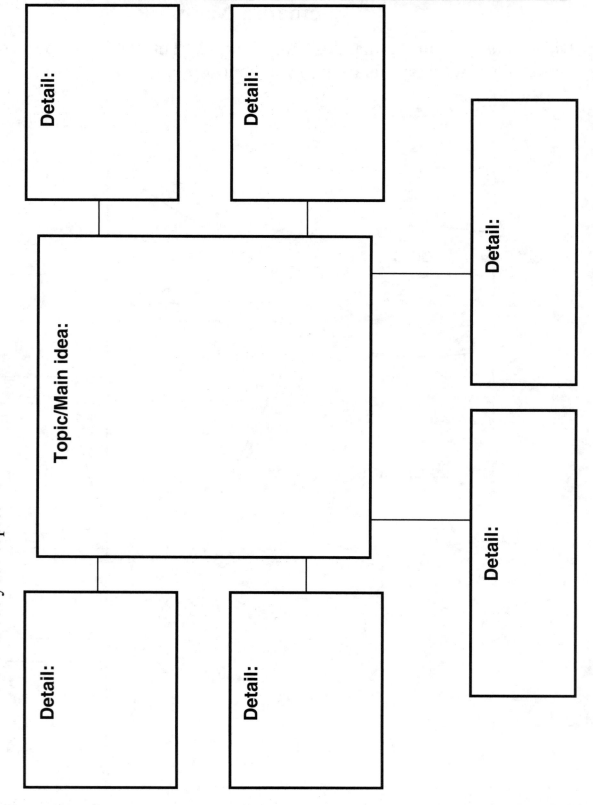

Detail:

Detail:

Detail:

Detail:

Detail:

Detail:

Topic/Main idea:

Determine Importance—
Main Idea and Supporting Details

Creative Mapping—Part 2

Directions: In the oval, draw a picture of the main idea of your book. In the boxes around your picture, write words or draw pictures that tell about your topic.

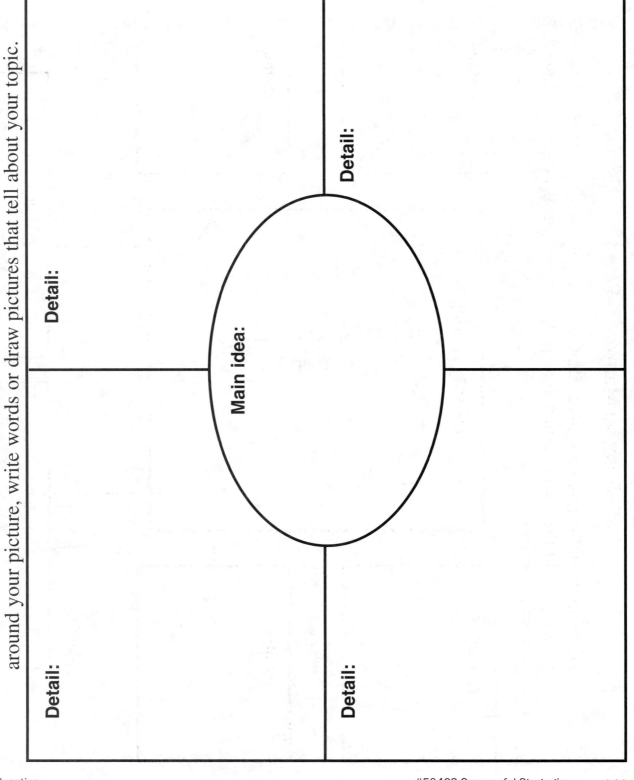

Detail:

Detail:

Main idea:

Detail:

Detail:

Determine Importance— Main Idea and Supporting Details

Main Idea Web

Directions: Write the main idea of your book in the center oval. Complete the web about the book.

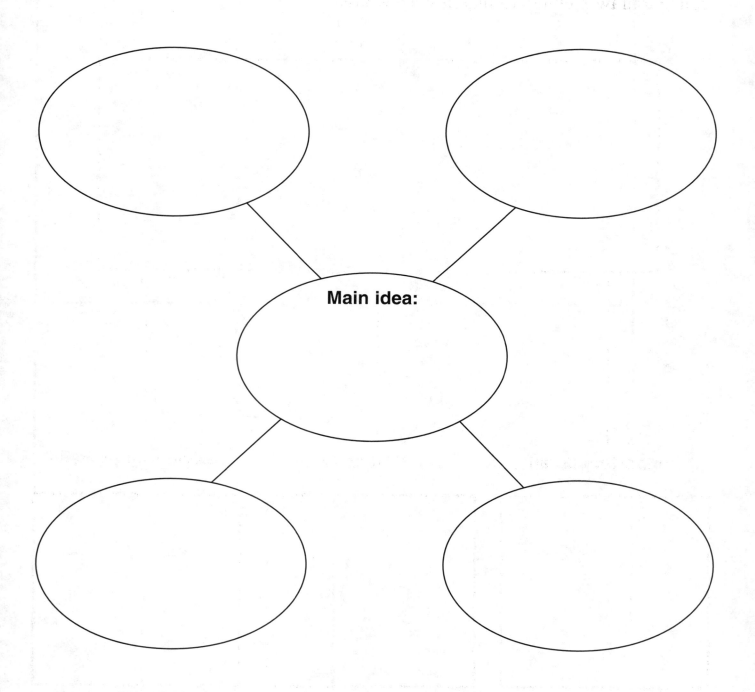

Main idea:

Determine Importance—
Main Idea and Supporting Details

Understanding the Main Idea

Directions: After reading, write the main idea in the box below and draw a picture of it. Write something you learned about the main idea in each box. You can draw pictures to match your words.

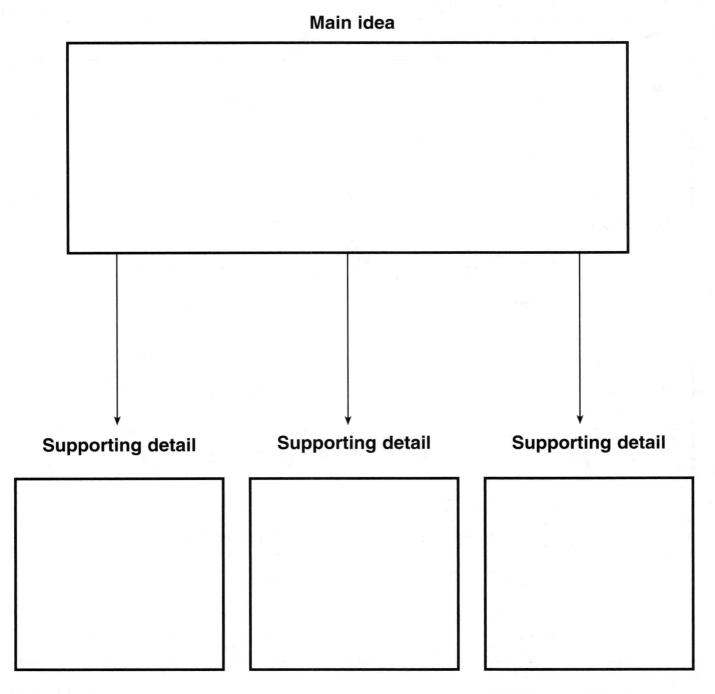

Main idea

Supporting detail

Supporting detail

Supporting detail

Determine Importance—
Main Idea and Supporting Details

Working with One Main Idea

Directions: Write the main idea in the top box. Then fill in four details that support the main idea.

Title: _____

Topic: _____

Main idea: _____

_____

_____

Supporting detail: _____

_____

_____

_____

_____

Supporting detail: _____

_____

_____

_____

_____

Supporting detail: _____

_____

_____

_____

_____

Supporting detail: _____

_____

_____

_____

_____

Determine Importance—
Main Idea and Supporting Details

Working with More Than One Main Idea

Directions: Find two main ideas in your book. Write one in each box. Write two details that support each main idea.

Title: _____

Topic: _____

Main idea 1: _____

_____

_____

Supporting detail: _____

_____

Supporting detail: _____

_____

Main idea 2: _____

_____

_____

Supporting detail: _____

_____

Supporting detail: _____

_____

Determine Importance—
Main Idea and Supporting Details

Think-Aloud Chart

Directions: Look at the cover of your book. Draw a picture of it on the book cover below. Then complete the statements in each box.

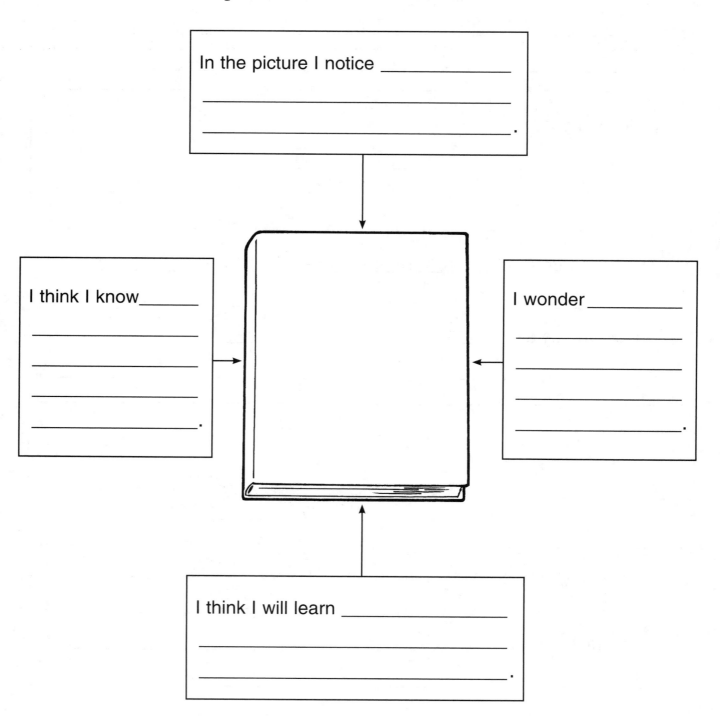

In the picture I notice _____

_____

_____ .

I think I know _____

_____

_____

_____ .

I wonder _____

_____

_____

_____ .

I think I will learn _____

_____

_____ .

Determine Importance— Main Idea and Supporting Details

Mini-Lesson: Finding the Main Idea 1

Directions: Read the paragraph below. Underline the main idea.

Jumping Frogs

Frogs have long, strong back legs.

They use their legs to dive and jump.

Some frogs can go as far as five feet in one jump!

Can you jump that far?

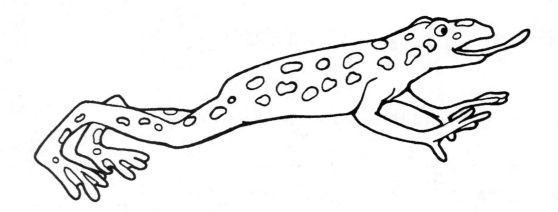

Determine Importance— Main Idea and Supporting Details

Mini-Lesson: Finding the Main Idea 2

Directions: Read the paragraph below. Think about the main idea. Then answer the questions.

Clouds

Look up at the sky and you see clouds. Clouds are made of tiny drops of water. Some clouds are white. They do not carry rain. Some clouds are dark. These carry rain and mean that a storm is near. If you see dark clouds, get out your umbrella!

1. What are clouds made of? _____

_____

2. How do you know if it is going to rain? _____

_____

3. What is the main idea in this paragraph? _____

_____

Determine Importance— Main Idea and Supporting Details

Mini-Lesson: Finding the Main Idea 3

Directions: Read the paragraph below. Then complete the activity.

Sea Turtles

Sea turtles are very good swimmers. They have flat shells that let them move fast in the water. Their legs are flat flippers with webs between the toes. These legs are not very good for walking, but they allow the sea turtle to swim many miles in a day.

1. Write the sentence that tells the main idea of the paragraph.

   _____

2. Write a sentence that gives a detail about the paragraph.

   _____

STRATEGIES AND SKILLS

Determine Importance—
Main Idea and Supporting Details

T-Chart

Directions: Write one main idea on each side of the chart. Below it, include a few examples of your main idea. Then fill in details under each main idea that support it.

Main Idea: _____	Main Idea: _____
Examples: _____	Examples: _____
Details 1. _____ 2. _____ 3. _____	**Details** 1. _____ 2. _____ 3. _____

Determine Importance— Text Structures

To be successful readers of nonfiction texts, students must use a variety of strategies to aid in their comprehension. However, many of the strategies that students have learned from fiction texts do not transfer to reading nonfiction. Most nonfiction texts do not have pictures that support the text, and the style of the text is formatted differently than a fiction text. Gone are the predictable words and patterns found in fiction books. Now students must learn to read unfamiliar vocabulary terms with little word-recognition support. The structure of a nonfiction text is unfamiliar. Students must learn new ways to understand what they are reading. Looking for patterns in the text is one of these ways.

Nonfiction Text Structures

Informational texts are organized in various ways. This organization helps readers understand and locate information in the text. Sometimes simple information may be presented first so readers can use it to build on more complex information. Other times, information is compared and contrasted. Sometimes a problem or idea is posed, or a question is asked, and then various solutions or strategies are given to solve that problem or idea. Knowing the structural patterns of nonfiction texts will help students fully comprehend nonfiction texts. Examples of nonfiction text structures are listed below.

- Chronological, Logical, or Sequential Order

- Compare and Contrast

- Cause and Effect

- Proposition and Support

- Progression of Ideas

Structural patterns are used in nonfiction text to arrange and connect ideas. Usually there are several structural patterns incorporated in the same text. Some nonfiction texts combine structural patterns, which often indicate a well-written text. Figuring out which structural pattern is being used in the text not only helps students understand the text but also allows them to comprehend the text at a higher level. Each type of text pattern listed on the following pages has key words to help students identify which pattern is being used. Identifying the type of text structure will help students better understand the text.

Determine Importance—
Text Structures

Nonfiction Text Structures *(cont.)*

Chronological, Logical, and Sequential Order: This type of text structure presents information in an organized manner. Directions are given in step-by-step order. You may find that some sequential structures have a narrative quality, but not always. This type of structure should be read like a narrative. Students should start at the beginning and read until the end of the text to clearly comprehend the ideas presented. Nonfiction writers sometimes present information in logical categories. This organization allows readers to skip to a selected topic without having to read all of the text. Often each topic builds from another topic within this structure. Readers must then search back in the text to find the information that will provide the background knowledge necessary to understand the topic. Signal words for this structure include the following:

first	after
next	when
then	finally
initially	preceding
before	following

Compare and Contrast: The writer using this structural pattern compares two people, ideas, or events, and shows how they are both similar and different. The writer usually states the topic or idea that organizes the text in a categorical structure. This organization helps readers clearly identify the topic and understand why the comparison is significant. The writer will also use description while comparing the two topics to make specific points. Signal words in a compare-and-contrast text include the following:

while	unlike	the same
yet	same	however
but	as opposed to	by contrast
rather	as well as	whereas
most	likewise	different than
either . . . or	on the other hand	similar to
like	although	similarly

Determine Importance—
Text Structures

Nonfiction Text Structures *(cont.)*

Cause and Effect: Cause and effect is a common structure of many nonfiction texts. The effect of something is what happens as a result of the cause. Introducing cause-and-effect signal words is a great way for students to learn how to recognize this text structure. This structure will be most familiar to students and will seem easier for them to understand because cause-and-effect structures are common in narrative fiction texts. Some of the signal words that students can look for include the following:

because of	may be due to	if . . . then	so that
as a result of	effects of	thus	this led to
in order to	therefore	since	then . . . so

Proposition and Support: In nonfiction texts, writers often present a problem or idea and then propose a solution or support for that idea. The problem or idea should be stated clearly and contain supporting details so that readers can understand the solution or support. The teacher should take the time to show students why the problem/idea and solution/support are important. When showing why this structure is important, examine cause and effect. Many problems and solutions are derived from cause-and-effect situations. In a problem-and-solution text, readers will see similar words used for cause and effect. In addition, they may see signal words such as the following:

purpose	leads one/me to conclude	the evidence is
consequently	a solution	a reason for
therefore	the problem	propose
as a result	the question	another
thereby	research shows	most important

Progression of Ideas: A writer using this structural pattern presents the ideas or events in the order in which they occur. An idea is taken from a beginning point to an end point through a logical sequence of events. The writer also uses details to support the key concepts. Readers will most likely see the following words with this text structure:

first	another	before
second	then	after
last	additionally	finally
next		

Determine Importance— Text Structures

The following strategies help introduce students to the structures of nonfiction text.

Strategy 1: Signal Words

Signal words and cue words are used to show how a text is organized as well as point out the valuable information that is being presented. One way to help students see the importance of these words is to enlarge a page of text that has numerous examples of signal or cue words. Students have copies of the text and a highlighter pen to skim the text for the selected words. Model this strategy several times using chart paper or an overhead projector before having students try to find the words on their own. This activity can also be done with the whole class by making a transparency of the text. The activity on page 159 can be used for this strategy. (Standards 5.2, 5.4, 5.6, 5.7, 7.1)

Strategy 2: Mix It Up

The teacher writes the following sequencing words—first, second, third, fourth—on 6-inch sentence strips. The class reads the words aloud. The teacher also writes the steps for a simple procedure on sentence strips. Together, the class reads each of these sentences. Then the teacher mixes up the word and sentence strips and gives a student one of the word strips to place next to the appropriate sentence. Here is an example for "Steps for Planting a Bean Seed." (Standard 8.5)

Steps for Planting a Bean Seed	
First	Put some soil in a cup.
Second	Place a bean in the cup and cover it with soil.
Third	Pour some water in the cup.
Fourth	Place the cup in a window.

Strategy 3: Time Line

Time lines are a great way to help younger students understand what happened in the text and when it happened. The essential feature of a time line is that the events are labeled and represented in sequence on a linear chart. Teachers can use a time line in different ways; they can write the events and have students label dates, or write the dates and have students label events. Practice this strategy many times because this is a new concept for young students. A template for a time line appears on page 160. (Standards 5.1, 7.1, 7.2, 7.3, 7.4)

Strategy 4: Comic Strips

Choose a comic strip that has a definite sequence to it. Cut the pictures apart. Students assemble the comic strip in the correct order. Then they write a paragraph explaining why they put it in the order they did, telling how they knew the correct order. Ask them to also write any key words from the comic strip that helped them determine the correct order. (Standards 5.1, 5.2, 5.6, 7.2, 7.3)

Determine Importance— Text Structures

Strategy 5: Flow Chart

Flow charts help students visualize a sequence of events. You can use this strategy to help students outline the sequence of a nonfiction chapter you are studying. This type of strategy can be used to tell a progression of ideas as well. To tell a sequence of events, make sure the students label the events in numerical order. Students can write the events in order or they can draw pictures to represent the ideas occurring in order. Use the activity on page 161 with this strategy. (Standards 5.1, 5.2, 7.1, 7.2)

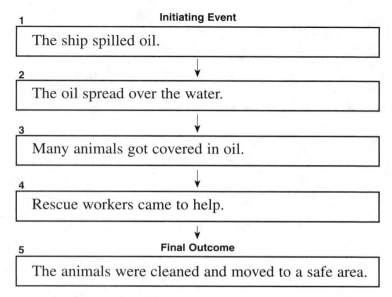

Initiating Event

1. The ship spilled oil.

2. The oil spread over the water.

3. Many animals got covered in oil.

4. Rescue workers came to help.

Final Outcome

5. The animals were cleaned and moved to a safe area.

Strategy 6: Put It in Order

An easy way to familiarize students with the vocabulary of chronological, logical, and sequential order is to have students verbally tell the steps for making a sandwich, playing a game, sharpening a pencil, etc. As students recite the steps, the teacher writes the key words for sequencing on the board or on a piece of chart paper. Have students highlight or underline the cue words for emphasis. A template to use with this strategy is on page 162. (Standards 5.6, 7.1, 7.2, 7.4)

An example is shown below (Task: how to make a peanut butter-and-jelly sandwich):

First, I get two pieces of bread.

Second, I get the peanut butter and jelly and a knife.

Third, I put the peanut butter and jelly on the bread.

Fourth, I put the pieces of bread together.

Last, I can eat the sandwich.

Strategy 7: Put It in Order 2

After reading and discussing a text, the teacher can call on students to share what they feel are the most important facts from the lesson. The teacher records each sentence on a sentence strip. Using a pocket chart, the teacher places the sentence strips into each pocket. The class reads each sentence strip. The teacher calls on individual students to find the sentence strip that should be first, second, third, etc. Once the sentence strips have been arranged in sequential order, students reread the sentences to make sure that the sequence is correct. If necessary, the teacher can call on a student to arrange the sentence strips to get the order correct. (Standards 7.1, 7.2, 8.2, 8.5)

Determine Importance— Text Structures

Strategy 8: Venn Diagram

Venn diagrams allow students to see the visual representation of common elements. A Venn diagram contains two circles that overlap in the center. First, students choose two things to compare, and then label each circle with one of these things. Then they list the ways that these things are different in the separate parts of the circles. Finally, in the overlapping section of the circles, students list the traits that the two things have in common. Use the template on page 163. (Standards 5.1, 7.1, 7.2, 7.3, 7.4)

Strategy 9: Alike and Different

This is another strategy to use when comparing and contrasting two things. Students first choose two things to compare and write each in the circle at the top of the page. Next, students will list four ways in which these two things are alike. Then, students list four ways in which the two things are different from each other. Use the activity on page 164 for this strategy. (Standards 5.1, 7.1, 7.2, 7.3, 7.4)

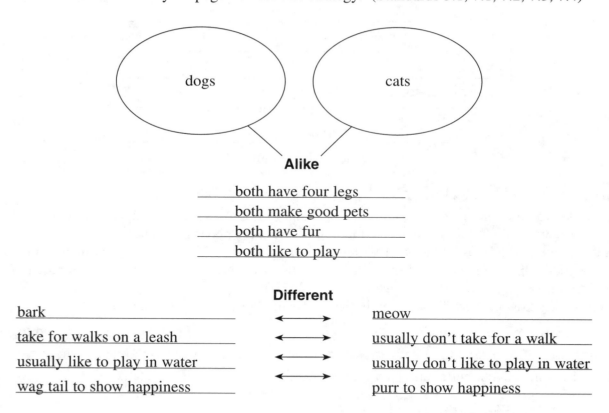

Strategy 10: Compare and Contrast H-Chart

Here is another strategy used to compare and contrast. Graphic organizers can help students visualize in different ways. The graphic organizer on page 165 uses the shape of an H. First, students choose two things to compare, and write each at the top of the sides of the H. Then, in the columns of the H, they list all the ways in which each thing is different from the other. Finally, in the center portion of the H, students list the ways in which the two things are the same. (Standards 5.1, 7.1, 7.2, 7.4)

Determine Importance— Text Structures

Strategy 11: Comparing and Contrasting Two Items

Charts can be used to compare and contrast two items, actions, or events. In the column on the far left, the teacher writes the areas of comparison for the two items, events, or topics being studied. At the top of the columns, the teacher labels the headings for the events being compared. Then the class generates facts that can be supported with evidence about the compared items. The supporting evidence might be from a certain page of a story, from an encyclopedia, or even from a video on the topic. A template for a compare-and-contrast chart is on page 166. An example of a completed chart is shown below. (Standards 5.1, 5.2, 7.1, 7.2, 7.3, 7.4, 8.2)

Topic: _____ Sports _____

	Baseball	Football
Equipment	bats gloves ball bases	elbow pads footballs shoulder pads
Clothing	baseball uniforms caps cleats	football uniforms helmets cleats
Fields	diamond-shaped field marked with four bases	100-yard field with markers every 10 yards

Strategy 12: Cause-and-Effect Chain

A cause-and-effect chain is a graphic organizer that helps students "see" the relationship between a cause and its effects. Students fill out the chain based on a nonfiction text that has been read in class. It is important to model this strategy many times until students feel comfortable with it. A template for this strategy is provided on page 167. An example is shown below:

Topic: _____ Bears _____

The Cause	The Effects

Campers leave candy bars in their tents. ⇨ Bears smell the candy bars and break into the tents. ⇨ Bears destroy the campgrounds. ⇨ Forest rangers have to track down the bears.

(Standards 5.1, 5.2, 7.1, 7.2, 7.3, 7.4)

Determine Importance—
Text Structures

Strategy 13: Cause-and-Effect Puzzle

Use the template on page 168 to fill in causes and effects. Students cut out the pieces and match the correct cause with the correct effect. An alternative to this activity is to give the students the blank template and have them find causes and effects from their nonfiction text. They can fill in the puzzle pieces, cut them apart, and then pair up with a partner. The partner can then try to match up the correct cause-and-effect puzzles. (Standards 5.1, 7.1, 7.2, 7.4, 8.2)

Strategy 14: Fishbone

Find the cause-and-effect statements in a nonfiction text and use the Fishbone graphic organizer on page 169 to display them. Students list the effect on the line across the fish, and the causes on the "bones" branching out from the main line. The fish can be colored, cut out, and displayed on a bulletin board. (Standards 5.1, 5.2, 7.1, 7.2, 7.3, 7.4)

Strategy 15: Support Your Ideas

First, find a nonfiction text that states a problem or idea and gives a solution or ways to implement the idea. Read this text together with your students. Provide copies of the text so that they can read it again with a partner. Working together, the students should find the proposed idea or problem. Then they should find statements that support a solution or the idea. Students should underline or highlight this information and then use the activity on page 170 to fill in the appropriate information. (Standards 5.2, 7.1, 7.2)

Strategy 16: Proposition and Support

Use the activity on page 171 for this activity. Students will need to read a piece of nonfiction text that uses the structure of proposition and support. This can be done as a class, then in small groups, then with partners, and eventually, individually. In the center oval, students write the idea or problem proposed in the text. In the surrounding ovals, the students write the supporting ideas, listing the page numbers where the support was found. (Standards 5.1, 5.2, 7.1, 7.2, 8.2, 8.5)

Strategy 17: Picture the Progression of Ideas

This strategy has students use pictures to tell the progression of ideas in a text. Students determine the main ideas of the text and the order in which they occur. Then students draw a picture of each of these ideas in the correct order. Use the activity on page 172 for this strategy. Students should also label the signal words under each picture, such as *first, second, third, next, then, last,* etc. The first and last words have been labeled for the students. (Standards 5.1, 5.2, 5.6, 7.1, 7.2, 8.5)

Determine Importance— Text Structures

Signal Words

Directions: Highlight the key words used in the text. Check off the words from the list below.

Book title:_____

Order

- ❏ numbering
- ❏ before
- ❏ finally
- ❏ next
- ❏ after
- ❏ then
- ❏ last

Compare and Contrast

- ❏ while
- ❏ most
- ❏ like
- ❏ either
- ❏ same
- ❏ different
- ❏ unlike

Cause and Effect

- ❏ because
- ❏ so
- ❏ reasons for
- ❏ due to
- ❏ as a result
- ❏ since
- ❏ then

Question and Answer

- ❏ answers who, what, when, where, why, how many
- ❏ it could be
- ❏ the best of

The text structure used is _____.

Determine Importance—
Text Structures

Time Line

Directions: On the time line below, write the events in the order that they occurred. Then write a sentence telling what happened.

Topic: _____

Observations, events, or milestones

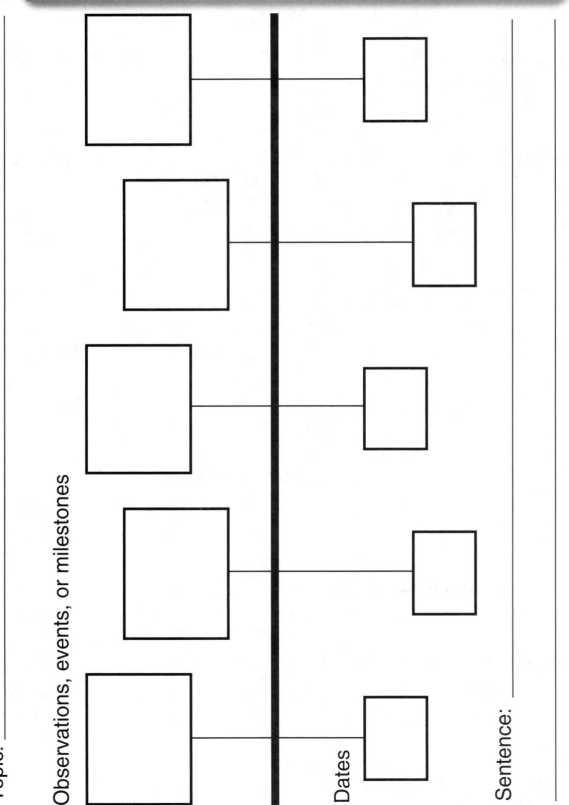

Dates

Sentence: _____

Determine Importance—
Text Structures

Flow Chart

Directions: First, choose the initiating event, or the event that started the chain of events. Write this event in the first box at the top of the page. Next, list each of the events in the order that they occurred, ending with the final outcome at the bottom of the page.

1   **Initiating event**

↓

2

↓

3

↓

4

↓

5   **Final Outcome**

Determine Importance— Text Structures

Put It in Order

Directions: Using the signal words below, write the steps for completing a task.

Task:_____

First, _____

_____

_____

Second, _____

_____

_____

Third, _____

_____

_____

Fourth, _____

_____

_____

Last,_____

_____

_____

Determine Importance—
Text Structures

Venn Diagram

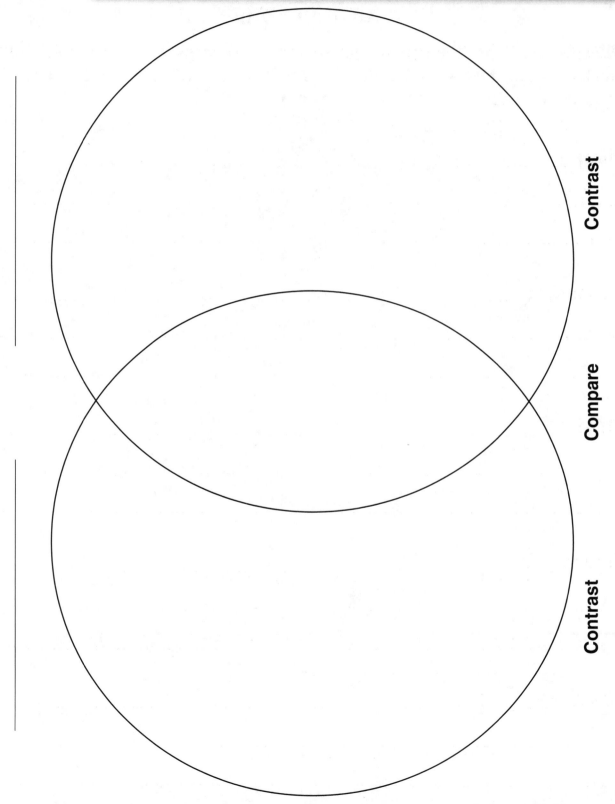

Contrast

Compare

Contrast

Determine Importance— Text Structures

Alike and Different

Directions: Write the two things you are comparing and contrasting in the ovals. Under the "Alike" column, write how the two are similar. Then list their differences in the two columns at the bottom.

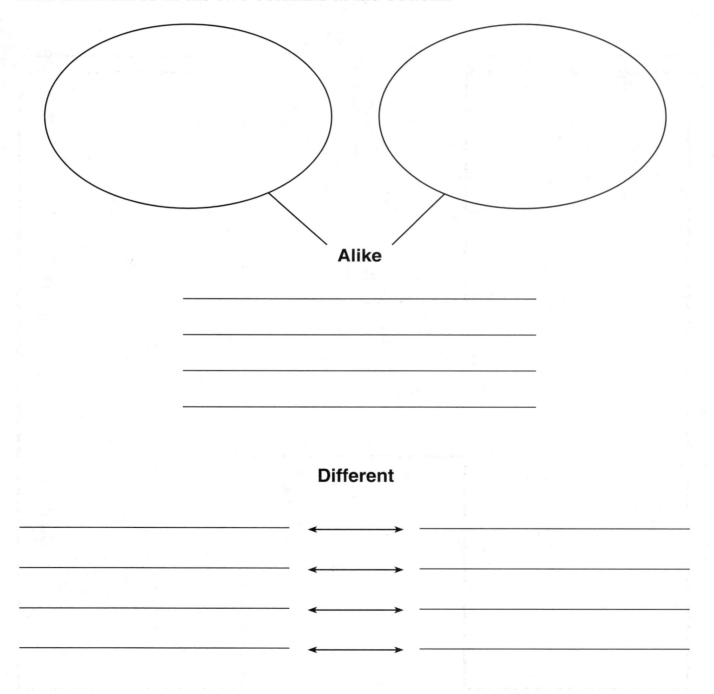

Alike

_____

_____

_____

_____

Different

Determine Importance—
Text Structures

Compare and Contrast H-Chart

Directions: Label each side of the H with the two things you are comparing and contrasting. Under each label, list the ways that each thing is different. In the center section of the H, list the ways that they are the same.

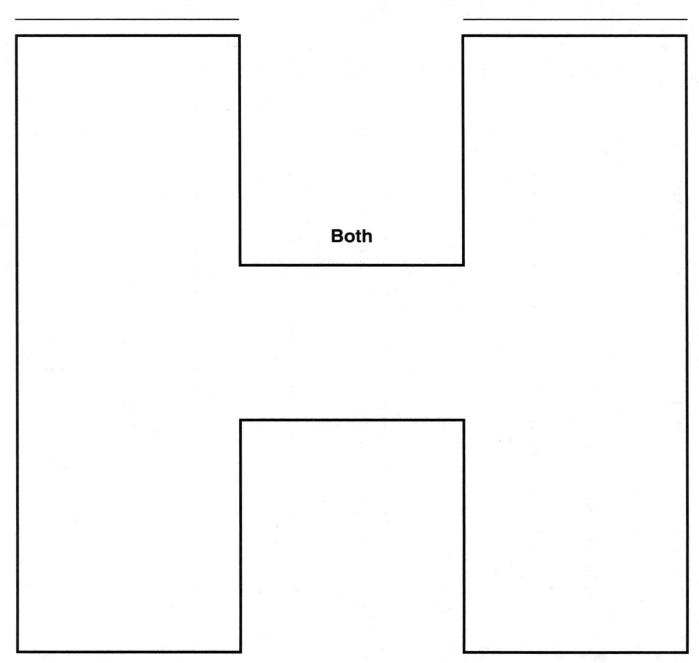

Both

Determine Importance— Text Structures

Comparing and Contrasting Two Items

Topic: _____

Items being compared →

Topics for comparison

Determine Importance—
Text Structures

Cause-and-Effect Chain

Topic: _____

The Effects
(results of the action)

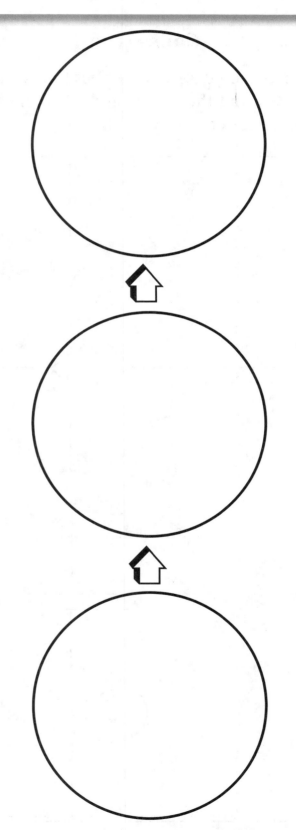

The Cause
(action or event)

Determine Importance—
Text Structures

Cause-and-Effect Puzzle

Directions: Read each cause and effect that your teacher has written on the puzzle pieces. Cut out the pieces and put them together correctly, matching each cause and effect correctly.

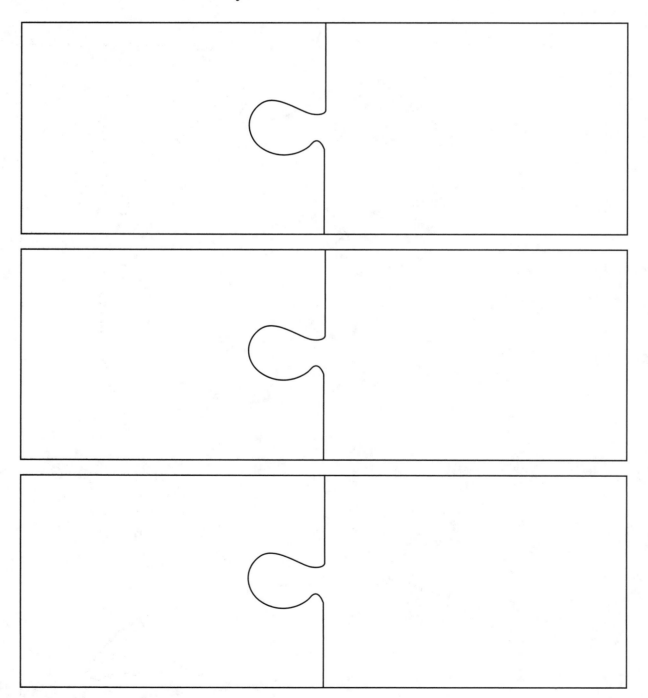

Determine Importance—
Text Structures

Fishbone

Directions: Choose the most important effect, or event, that happens in your nonfiction text. Write this effect on the line labeled "Effect." Then find the four most important things that caused this effect. Write each of these on a line that says "Cause."

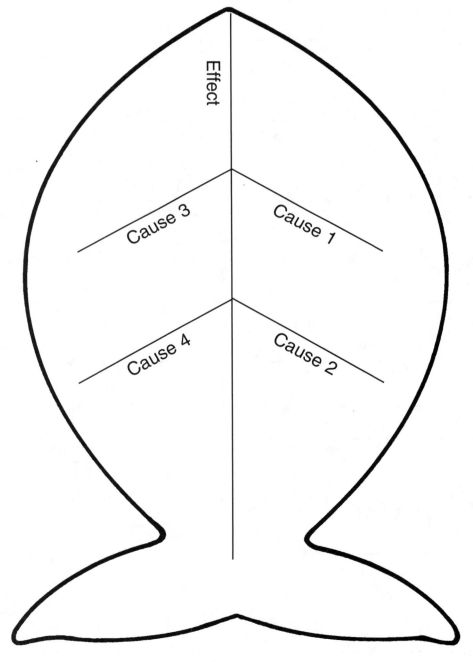

Determine Importance—
Text Structures

Support Your Ideas

Directions: Fill in the information from the text. First, find the main idea or problem stated in the text and write it on the lines next to "Proposition Stated." Then find three supporting ideas or solutions from the text and write them on the lines below. If you need more room, use the back of this sheet.

Proposition Stated: _____

_____

_____

Support:

1. _____

_____

_____

2. _____

_____

_____

3. _____

_____

_____

Determine Importance—
Text Structures

Proposition and Support

Directions: In the middle oval, labeled "Proposition," write the proposed idea or problem from your nonfiction text. Then, in each of the "Support" ovals, write the supporting ideas or solutions. Be sure to list the page number under each oval where you found the "Support" in your text.

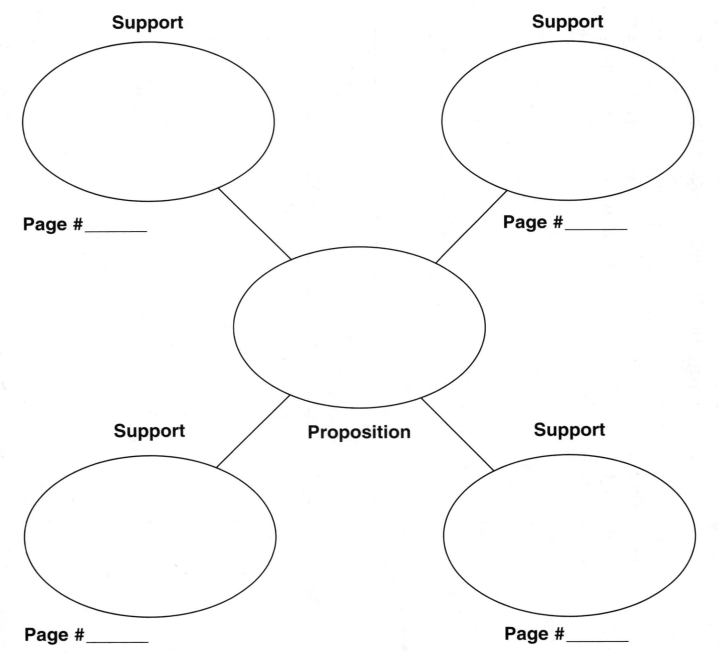

Support

Support

Page #_____

Page #_____

Support

Proposition

Support

Page #_____

Page #_____

Determine Importance—
Text Structures

Picture the Progression of Ideas

Directions: First, decide on the order of ideas in the nonfiction text that you have read. Then, using the boxes below, draw pictures of each of the ideas in order from first to last. Label the rest of the boxes with signal words. The first and last boxes have been labeled for you.

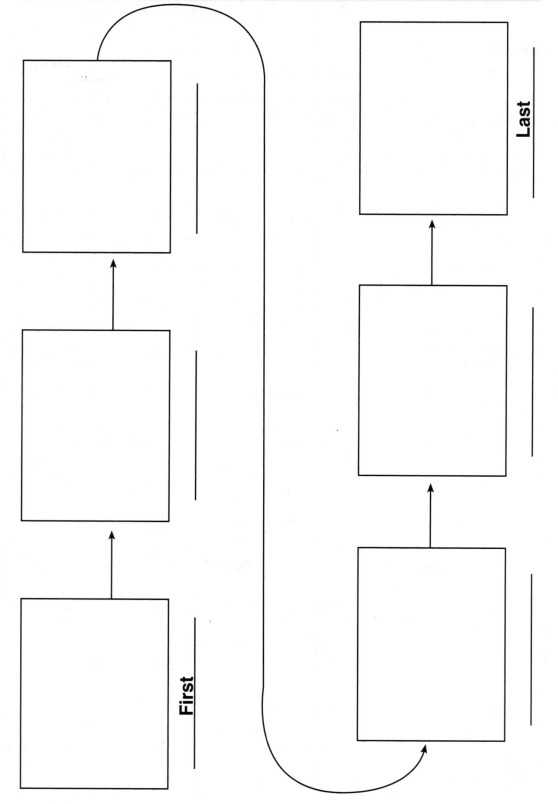

First

Last

Determine Importance— Text Organizers

Text organizers are ways of organizing information from the text into some type of order. Most nonfiction texts present information in a variety of ways, and they use things like indexes, tables of contents, chapter titles, and headings to help students find specific information. Expository texts require students to classify, explain, and find relationships within the text. Reading nonfiction texts must be done slowly and deliberately in order to grasp the concepts. Students are expected to understand many new concepts and specialized vocabulary. They must also interpret graphic aids such as graphs, maps, and charts. Diagrams often replace pictures that once supported the text. Nonfiction texts have headings and bold words—a structure that is new to students. Knowing how to recognize the features of nonfiction text will help students comprehend the text more successfully.

Features of Informational Texts

Just as informational texts have many different structures, they also have many different features. Being able to identify the features of a text will help students know what to look for to better understand the text they are reading.

Print Features: These features allow readers to know the patterns of the nonfiction text. Print features are used to guide readers through the patterns of organization. Research has shown that when readers know the patterns of a text, they understand the materials more easily. Print features include chapter titles, headings, subheadings, font sizes, bullets, italics, bold print, colored text, cue words, summary sentences, and phrases.

Chapter titles help guide readers to the categories the writer used to frame the book. Chapter titles also outline the sequence of the text. Titles, headings, and subheadings help readers find important information that may also be presented in different font sizes, italics, bold print, bullets, and colored text. The teacher should point out that the author uses these features to tell readers that the information is important.

Labels and captions with illustrations also provide readers with important information.

Cue words and phrases are signals for readers to read carefully. When readers see these phrases, they should take note of the information presented. Cue words and phrases include the following: *for example, in conclusion, therefore, for instance, most important, on the other hand, in fact, but,* and *such as.*

Determine Importance— Text Organizers

Features of Informational Texts *(cont.)*

Headings, topics, and summary sentences are all part of the text's overall structure and format. The information presented in nonfiction texts is divided into smaller chunks through the use of headings, subheadings, and topics. The paragraphs in each section are devoted to one aspect of the specific topic. By breaking the information into logical parts, students are then able to select the sections that they need to read and would like to learn more about. Summary sentences are a very important feature of nonfiction text. Summary sentences are found at the end of the paragraph and/or chapter and succinctly clarify the important concepts and ideas presented in the paragraph or chapter. This means that students can use text organizers to find information quickly without having to read every word on the page.

Graphic features present information in a specific way. Examples are diagrams, sketches, maps, charts, graphs, tables, cross-sectional drawings or views, time lines, flow charts, and other figures. In order to understand information presented graphically, students must first know how to interpret it. Teachers should look ahead to be sure students know how to interpret the graphic aids that are in the text they are reading. Students need to learn to obtain information from visual graphics such as photographs, illustrations, charts, diagrams, and bold type. These graphic features are used to capture students' attention and enhance their comprehension of the topic. The graphic features let students know that important information is being presented.

These features play an important role in enhancing reading comprehension. They can be used before, during, and after reading to show relationships between the words on the page and the whole idea being presented. Illustrations may be black-and-white drawings or photographs. Some photographs will be colorful and will capture readers' attention. Most drawings are accompanied by captions that explain the picture. When informational texts use illustrations, it is important to be sure that they are accurate and authentic because the illustrations carry the meaning of the text. It is also important for students to read the captions that accompany these graphic features—they also provide important information. It is possible for students to learn the same amount by looking at a picture and reading a caption as they would from reading an entire page of text.

Before reading a new text with students, take the time to preview and familiarize them with the graphic features used in the material. This will activate their prior knowledge on the topic, provide a glimpse into what they will be learning about, and highlight the text organizers being used.

Determine Importance— Text Organizers

Strategy 1: Print Features T-Graph

To introduce the concept of print features and concurrently assess what students know, the class can scan a nonfiction text and search for any changes in typeface. Students do not read the text, but simply look for any print variation. Students can have their own copies of the text or a transparency can be made for the whole class to read together. Model how to use this strategy several times before having students try it on their own. It is recommended that the teacher first model the strategy, then have the whole class participate. Then, when students are feeling more comfortable, they can try the activity in small groups. After the small groups have mastered the activity, the teacher can pair up students to try it. Once the teacher feels students are very comfortable with this strategy, students can try the activity independently.

The teacher makes a T-graph on chart paper. Students point out the types of print features (e.g., bold, colored print, italics) used while the teacher writes the print feature in the left column and the words or sentences emphasized by the feature in the right column of the graph. (See activity on page 180.) Students then make predictions about the text based on these observations. The teacher asks, "What clues do the print features give about the important information that will be in the text?" After reading the text, the class discusses the accuracy of their predictions and the effectiveness of the author's choice of print features. When students answer comprehension questions about the text or use the text to write reports, the teacher can remind them to use the print features graph. While introducing this concept, the teacher should pay attention to the information students are giving. It might be helpful to have a class list and quickly make notations about those students who seem to understand the importance of print features and how they work, and those students who do not. (Standards 5.1, 5.2, 7.1, 8.2, 8.5) The following is a sample T-Graph on print features:

Print Features	Words Emphasized
bold print	**blue**
bullets	• red
italics	*orange*

Strategy 2: Highlighting

One way to help students see the importance of key words is to enlarge a page of text that has numerous examples of signal or cue words. Students have copies of the text and highlighter pens to use while skimming the text for the selected words. This activity can also be done with the whole class by making a transparency of the text. Model this strategy several times with the whole class. At first, the teacher can model it by thinking out loud while completing each step. Then, students can use the overhead projector to show their classmates what to highlight. After students have had practice with this strategy, place them in small groups to work on the strategy collaboratively. (Standards 5.4, 5.6, 7.1)

Determine Importance— Text Organizers

Strategy 3: Previewing the Text

Before reading a new text with students, the teacher takes time to preview and familiarize students with the graphic features used in the material. This preview will activate students' prior knowledge on the topic, provide a glimpse into what they will be learning, and highlight the text structure being used. Some suggestions for previewing the graphic features are:

- to discuss the information presented on the charts and diagrams
- to read the captions under each illustration or photograph
- to discuss the maps, cutaways, tables, etc.

The activity on page 181 can be used for this strategy. (Standards 5.2, 7.1, 7.4)

Strategy 4: Chapter Overview

The teacher makes sure that each student or pair of students has a copy of the class textbook. Together, the students and teacher scan the textbook to find answers to questions about the text. The teacher has written these questions on chart paper ahead of time and reads them to students. Use questions such as:

1. What is the title of the chapter?
2. What are the headings in this chapter?
3. What are the subheadings in this chapter?
4. What words appear in bold, italics, or colored print?
5. Why do you think these words appear the way they do?
6. Are there any illustrations or photographs? Tell what they are.

This strategy helps students become familiar with a chapter in a textbook without actually reading the chapter. When it comes time to read the chapter, students will know what to expect and, therefore, will have increased comprehension. Allow plenty of exploration time with the textbooks so that students can feel comfortable and familiar with them. After modeling this strategy, use the activity on page 182. (Standards 5.2, 7.1, 8.2)

Strategy 5: Web Organizer

Webs are very useful when trying to organize information. A web helps students locate information in a nonfiction text before reading it. The web organizer on page 183 can be modeled with the class. Teacher and students look at the title of the chapter and discuss the main idea of the chapter. The main idea goes in the center of the web. Next, students go through the chapter to find any subheadings that pertain to the main idea. After they have found the subheadings, they read through the chapter, noting any print features such as cue words, phrases, bold, or italics, and adding those to the web. Now that students have organized and located the important parts of the text, they are ready to read for meaning. (Standards 5.1, 5.2, 5.4, 5.6, 7.1, 7.2)

Determine Importance— Text Organizers

Strategy 6: Graphics and Captions

Choose a chapter of nonfiction text to read with students. Use the activity on page 184 for this strategy. Have them write the title of the chapter and then look at the graphic features in the chapter. Students should list all of the types of graphic features found in the chapter. Then they should write all of the captions that were written with the graphic features. After that, they should write a sentence that tells the main idea of the chapter. Finally, they should read the text in the chapter to see if their prediction was correct. (Standards 5.2, 5.7, 7.2, 7.3)

Strategy 7: Two-Column Note Taking

When using this strategy it is important to find a text that has many headings and subheadings and many details that give information about the topic. Begin by using the template for Two-Column Note Taking found on page 185. The page is divided into two parts, titled "Topic" and "Details." Write the first heading in the left-hand column. List some details about that heading from the reading in the right-hand column. Then write the first subheading you come to in the left-hand column. Read the text that follows that subheading and list some details in the right-hand column.

Continue in this manner until you reach the end of the page, chapter, or section you have chosen. This strategy should definitely be modeled several times as a whole class before having students try to do it independently. As students get more proficient with this strategy, increase the difficulty level of the text. (Standards 5.2, 7.1, 7.2, 8.5)

Strategy 8: Three-Column Note Taking

After students are comfortable using two-column note taking, it is time to introduce a third column. Use the Three-Column template on page 186. The third column, "Response," gives students a place to write their personal responses to the reading. A personal response can be students' feelings, questions, inferences, or thoughts about what they are reading. When students can make a connection to the text, they will remember what was read and achieve a deeper level of understanding. (Standards 5.2, 7.1, 7.2, 7.4, 8.5)

Strategy 9: What Does It Say?

The teacher chooses a piece of text that contains at least one graphic feature. The activity on page 187 works well for this strategy. Students choose a graphic feature from this text and draw a picture of it in the box. Then they should write three sentences explaining the information that is presented in the graphic. Model this strategy several times with the entire class. Then place students in small groups to give them additional practice. (Standards 5.2, 7.1, 7.2, 7.3, 8.5)

Determine Importance— Text Organizers

Strategy 10: Chapter Titles

The teacher chooses a book that contains several chapters and reads the title of the book to students. On chart paper, the teacher lists the chapter titles of the book. The class discusses each chapter title and its meaning, and brainstorms ideas for what each chapter might be about. These ideas are listed on chart paper next to each of the titles. Then the class predicts what the main idea of the book might be. The activity on page 188 is a guide to this strategy. (Standards 5.1, 5.2, 7.1)

Strategy 11: Text Organizer Scavenger Hunt

The teacher divides students into groups of four and gives them a time limit of 5–10 minutes, depending on the maturity/ability of the group and the complexity of the text. Using the template on page 189 as a guide, students identify each text organizer in the book. The first group to finish the scavenger hunt earns a reward. (Standards 5.2, 7.1, 7.2)

Strategy 12: Buddy Reading

Interacting with peers is an essential component for developing proficiency in reading. Students find group work highly motivating, and when structured, the teacher can greatly maximize students' learning. Students work with a partner to complete the Buddy Reading activity (page 190) to identify how one text organizer reveals important information and informs them about the main idea. It is imperative that students are continually directed to think about how the content of the text and the text organizers are intended to work together to teach them about the main idea. (Standards 5.2, 7.1, 7.2, 7.3, 8.5)

Strategy 13: Using the Newspaper

Using a section from a local newspaper, the school's newspaper, or a parent newsletter, students locate the title of the section. Next, they list the headlines of the articles that appear in that section. The class discusses why the editor chose to put these articles in that particular section. Then students predict what they think each of the articles will be about, based on the headlines. (Standards 5.2, 7.1)

Determine Importance— Text Organizers

Strategy 14: SQ3R

SQ3R stands for **Survey**, **Question**, **Read**, **Recite**, and **Review**. This is a very detailed strategy and needs to be modeled many times. It is a good idea to use this strategy in a shared-reading situation several times until students feel comfortable with it.

Survey involves scanning the text for information. Scanning means looking at titles, headings, subheadings, pictures, graphs, print features, etc. The purpose of surveying is to get an overview of the material that is about to be presented.

Question means to turn each heading and subheading into a question. Questions set a purpose for reading and help students focus on what they are about to read.

Reading the text must be done carefully so as not to miss any information.

Recite means to retell the information either verbally or in writing.

Review is a time for students to take a few moments to recall what they have read.

This strategy needs to be modeled extensively before allowing students to do it independently. When modeling this strategy, the teacher may want to divide the class into groups of four, assigning a task to each member using the activity on page 191. One group member surveys, another questions, all students read, a third member recites, and the last member reviews the material. Be sure to break up the reading material into small enough chunks so students do not become overwhelmed. Switch roles with each new heading or piece of reading material. (Standards 5.2, 7.1, 7.3, 8.5)

Strategy 15: Outline

For this activity, students will make an outline showing the text organizers from their nonfiction text. Use the activity on page 192 for this strategy. Tell the students that they will use this activity to organize their thoughts about a chapter they are reading. Students should write the title, heading, and subheading of the chapter on the lines. Then the students should read the entire chapter. After reading the chapter, students should determine the main idea and write this also. Finally, they should write some of the supporting details and key words or phrases from the chapter that helped them determine the main idea. (Standards 5.1, 5.2, 5.6, 7.1, 7.2, 7.3)

Strategy 16: Pyramid

This strategy allows students to write the most important information from the chapter in a graphic organizer to help them remember the information. Use the activity on page 193 for this strategy. First, have students write the chapter title in the top of the pyramid. Then students should read the entire chapter. After reading the chapter, students need to determine the main idea and write this in the next section of the pyramid. Then the students should list the subheadings of the chapter in the next section of the pyramid. Finally, students should list any other details and key words from the chapter that helped them to locate the main idea. (Standards 5.1, 5.2, 7.1, 7.2, 8.5)

Determine Importance— Text Organizers

Print Features T-Graph

Directions: List the types of features the author used in the left column and the words that were emphasized in the right column. In your own words, write what you think the text means. Then write a sentence that tells the conclusion. Is there anything you learned from the text that wasn't written there?

Print features:

- change in font
- colored print
- italicized words
- bold print
- bullets

Print features	Words emphasized

Conclusions (inferences): _____

_____

_____

_____

_____

Determine Importance— Text Organizers

Previewing the Text

Directions: Answer the following questions before reading the book.

Book title:_____

1. Check off the graphic features used in the book.

    _____ diagrams

    _____ maps

    _____ photographs

    _____ illustrations

    _____ charts

    _____ other: _____

2. Find examples of the following:

    A word written in italics: _____ on page _____

    A word written in bold print: _____ on page _____

    A word that is larger than other words on the page: _____
    on page _____

    A chapter title:_____ on page _____

    A heading or subheading: _____
    on page _____

3. What do you think this book will be about? Why do you think so?

    _____

    _____

    _____

Determine Importance— Text Organizers

Chapter Overview

Directions: Scan the textbook chapter to find the answers to the following questions. Write your answers on the lines.

1. What is the title of the chapter? _____

2. List the headings in this chapter. _____

   _____

   _____

3. List the subheadings in this chapter. _____

   _____

   _____

4. What words appear in bold, italics, or colored print? _____

   _____

   _____

5. Why do you think these words appear the way they do? _____

   _____

   _____

6. Are there any illustrations or photographs? _____ What are they?

   _____

   _____

Determine Importance—
Text Organizers

Web Organizer

Directions: Write the chapter title below. Determine the main idea of the chapter and write it in the center circle. Find subheadings in the chapter that support the main idea. Write each one in a circle labeled "Subheading." Next, read the subheadings to find print features such as cue words, bold, italics, etc. Write these on the lines extending from the "Subheading" circles.

Chapter title: _____

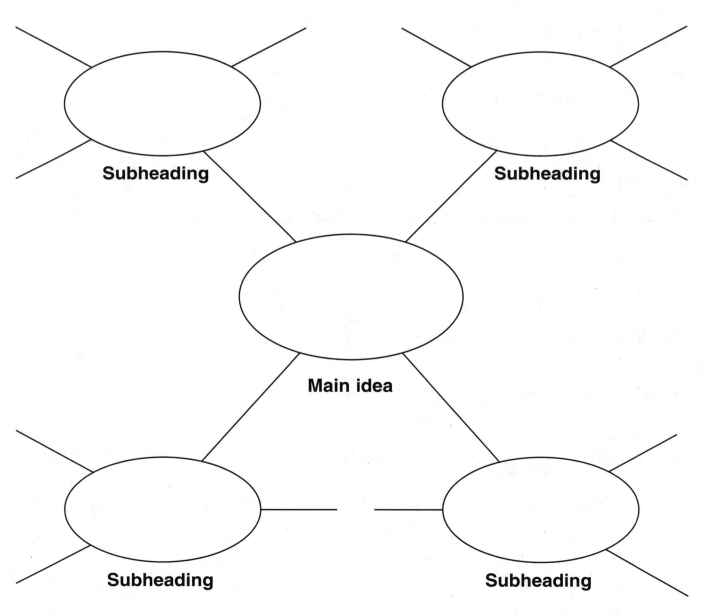

Determine Importance— Text Organizers

Graphics and Captions

Directions: Write the title of the chapter on the line below. Look at the graphic features in the chapter. List all the types of graphic features found in the chapter. Write all the captions that were written with the graphic features. Write a sentence that predicts the main idea of the chapter. Now read the text in the chapter to see if your prediction was correct.

Title of chapter: _____

Types of graphic features: _____

_____

_____

_____

Captions: _____

_____

_____

_____

_____

_____

Main idea prediction: _____

_____

_____

_____

_____

Determine Importance—
Text Organizers

Two-Column Note Taking

Directions: Read the text your teacher has chosen for you. Decide what the topic is and write it in the column labeled "Topic." Next, look for details that support the topic and write them in the column labeled "Details."

Topic	Details

Determine Importance— Text Organizers

Three-Column Note Taking

Directions: Read the text your teacher has chosen for you. Decide what the topic is and write it in the column labeled "Topic." Next, look for details that support the topic and write them in the column labeled "Details." In the column labeled "Response," write your own feelings, questions, or thoughts about what you read.

Topic	Details	Response

Determine Importance—
Text Organizers

What Does It Say?

Directions: Choose a graphic feature from your book and draw it below. Make a list of the different facts that can be learned from reading this graphic feature.

Book title:_____

1. _____

2. _____

3. _____

Determine Importance—
Text Organizers

Chapter Titles

Directions: List the chapter titles in your book. Name something you will learn in each chapter. Use the chapter titles to help you figure out the main idea of the book and write it at the bottom of the page.

1. Chapter title: _____

   I will learn _____

2. Chapter title: _____

   I will learn _____

3. Chapter title: _____

   I will learn _____

4. Chapter title: _____

   I will learn _____

5. Chapter title: _____

   I will learn _____

The main idea is _____

_____

Determine Importance—
Text Organizers

Text Organizer Scavenger Hunt

Directions: Find all of the text organizers in your book and write them below. List as many as you can find!

Determine Importance— Text Organizers

Buddy Reading

Directions: With a partner, explain how text organizers show important facts or the main idea in text.

Buddy #1: Tell about a text organizer.

_____

_____

Buddy #1: Does the text organizer show important facts? Explain.

_____

_____

Buddy #2: Tell about a text organizer.

_____

_____

Buddy #2: Does the text organizer tell you more about the main idea of the text? Explain.

_____

_____

Determine Importance— Text Organizers

SQ3R

Directions: Follow the directions for each section below.

Survey the text. Write what you saw.

_____

_____

_____

Questions. Change the headings in the text into questions.

_____

_____

_____

Read the text selection carefully.

Recite. Write or tell about what you read.

_____

_____

_____

_____

Review. Look over what you wrote in the **Recite** section above. Did you forget anything? Add it here.

_____

_____

_____

_____

Determine Importance— Text Organizers

Outline

Directions: Use this outline to organize your thoughts about a chapter you are reading. Write the title, heading, and subheading of the chapter on the lines below. Then read the entire chapter. Determine the main idea and write this also. Write some of the supporting details and key words from the chapter that helped you figure out the main idea.

I. Title _____

  A. Heading

    _____

  B. Subheading

    _____

  C. Main idea

    _____

    _____

    1. Supporting details

      _____

      _____

      _____

    2. Key words or phrases

      _____

      _____

      _____

Determine Importance— Text Organizers

Pyramid

Directions: First write the chapter title in the top of the pyramid. Then read the entire chapter. Determine the main idea and write this in the next section of the pyramid. Then list the subheadings of the chapter in the next section of the pyramid. Then list any other details and key words from the chapter that helped you determine the main idea.

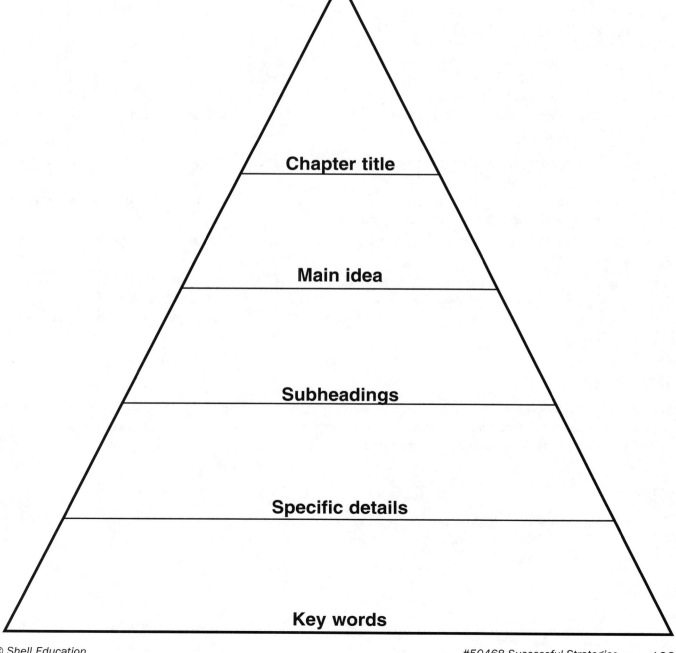

Determine Importance—Using Parts of the Book

Nonfiction texts have many structural features that help students locate specific information on a topic. Most nonfiction texts contain similar basic structural elements. Two parts of a book that students need to learn to use in second grade in order to locate important information are the table of contents and the index. When students have acquired the necessary skills of using a table of contents and an index, they will save time locating information. More challenging parts of the book that students can learn about are the title page, copyright page, dedication page, appendix, glossary, and preface. All parts of the book can help students determine what is important in a text.

Locating Information

Locating information is an important strategy in comprehending nonfiction texts. When finding information in nonfiction texts, students are required to use different strategies from the ones they use to understand fiction texts. Fiction texts do not include the parts of a book such as table of contents, glossaries, and indexes that are found in nonfiction texts. In order to locate information in nonfiction texts, students must:

- Formulate a goal. Students must have a question about the information in the text and need or want to find the answer.
- Select an appropriate tool to find the answer. Students must know where to locate the information in an index, glossary, table of contents, preface, etc.
- Use the appropriate tool to pull out the information. Students need to identify the important facts and extract them from the text.

A nonfiction book can be divided into three main sections. The three sections are the front section, the body of the text, and the back section. The front section contains the title page, copyright page, preface, table of contents, and sometimes a list of illustrations. These pages are usually numbered with lowercase Roman numerals.

Title Page

The first page is called the title page. The title page contains the complete title of the book, the author's name, the publisher's name, and the place of publication. The copyright page comes right after the title page. This page tells the year the book was published and the copyright owner's name.

Copyright

The copyright date is usually the same as the date of publication. It is important for students to check the copyright date because information can become outdated.

Determine Importance— Using Parts of the Book

Dedication

The copyright page might also have a short dedication. A dedication is one way that authors can thank the people who have played an important part in their life, education, and career, or in writing the book.

The preface, acknowledgements, and foreword can be used in very similar ways. A textbook might have only one of these features or it might have all of them. Each one, though, serves a different purpose.

Acknowledgements

In the acknowledgements, authors can thank the people who have been supportive of their research or have helped in their writing efforts. The acknowledgments can be several pages in length.

Foreword

The foreword is a statement written by someone other than the author. The foreword is used to give the text more authority. Someone who is considered to be an expert on the topic of the book might write the foreword.

Preface

The preface is located at the beginning of the book and comes before the table of contents. Preface means "to speak beforehand." The preface can be short (less than a page) or as long as several pages. The preface is very similar to the introduction. The first sentences tell why the book was written. It provides students with a general overview of the information that will be covered in the body of the text and provides any necessary background information on the topic.

Title

The title of the book can be used to activate students' prior knowledge on the topic and stimulate their interest in reading a book. Students should be encouraged to examine the cover of the book to generate predictions, interest, and questions about the topic.

List of Illustrations

A list of illustrations is often included in nonfiction books. It provides information about the different types of graphic materials that can be found in the book. The list of illustrations provides the title of the illustration and the page number where it can be found. Illustrations can be maps, letters, charts, diagrams, photos, tables, drawings, etc. These graphics are all important features of nonfiction texts and help to clarify the information by presenting it in a format other than text. They can enhance students' understandings of the text and serve as an aid in remembering and recalling the information.

Determine Importance— Using Parts of the Book

Table of Contents

The table of contents is located at the front of the book. The table of contents serves as a guide for the whole text, indicates how the information will be organized in the text, and tells students where additional information on the topic can be found. The table of contents divides the information presented in the book into smaller sections. These divisions are called chapters. Each chapter provides information on one specific topic or subject. Second-graders may have limited exposure to using a table of contents. For instance, they may be able to locate the title of a particular story and the page on which it begins. Throughout the year, students will need in-depth instruction in using a table of contents.

Body

The body of the book is the main section. The body is also called the text of the book. This is the section where the information outlined in the introduction is described more fully and in greater detail. The body of the book is usually made up of different chapters. Each chapter provides information on one specific aspect of the topic. Each chapter is further divided into smaller sections through the use of headings, subheadings, and paragraphs. After the body of the book comes the end section, which contains the appendix, glossary, bibliography, and index.

Appendix

The appendix is a supplemental tool that supports and expands upon a character, topic, subject, or information presented in the body of the work. The appendix provides additional information in the form of maps, diagrams, copies of letters, official documents, charts, forms, and/or illustrations. These items can serve as important reference tools for students as they seek out new information and integrate it with their prior knowledge.

Glossary

The glossary is a type of specialized dictionary. Like a dictionary, the words are listed in alphabetical order. The glossary defines technical, foreign, or special terms and words used in the body of the text. The glossary might also show how the words are pronounced.

Bibliography

The bibliography lists books or articles that were used by the author in writing the book. Each entry provides the title, author's name, place of publication, publisher's name, and the date of publication.

Index

The layout of an index may be more familiar to students who have had previous experience with alphabetizing. When teaching how to use an index, the teacher should point out that information is arranged by topics and subtopics. The teachers should also explain any other notations that may accompany the topics and subtopics, such as numbers and abbreviations. After students are familiar with the structure, the teacher should focus instruction on using an index to locate information.

Determine Importance—Using Parts of the Book

Strategy 1: Table of Contents

Use the activity on page 199 to teach students how to find facts using their table of contents. This strategy is a good review after practicing using the table of contents for several lessons. Based on the information provided in the table of contents, students write two questions at the bottom of the page that they would like to have answered by their reading. This serves to establish a purpose for reading the text. (Standards 5.2, 8.2)

Strategy 2: Create a Table of Contents

Use the activity on page 200 for this strategy. Have students use a nonfiction book that has chapters. Without looking at the existing table of contents (if there is one), students create their own tables of contents using the rest of the book as a guide. After students create their own tables of contents, have them compare it to the existing one in the book. Were they as thorough or more thorough than the existing one? Did they add anything important that the publisher left out? (Standards 5.2, 7.1, 8.2)

Strategy 3: Using the Newspaper

Use local newspapers to teach how to use a table of contents. Before using this strategy, preview the paper for content. Use the template on page 201 after you have modeled lessons on tables of contents. This strategy allows students to see how useful a table of contents can be even outside the classroom. (Standards 5.2, 7.1)

Strategy 4: Asking Questions

Using the activity on page 202, students will read the table of contents and then write three questions about it. They will also make an answer key for their questions. Next, students trade papers with other students to see if the questions can be answered. This activity shows whether students really understand the purpose of a table of contents. (Standards 5.2, 7.1, 7.2, 8.2, 8.5)

Strategy 5: Design a Book Cover

For this strategy, students will demonstrate their knowledge of book parts by designing a nonfiction book cover. Students should include:

- the title of the book
- the author's name
- the illustrator's name
- a picture

The teacher allows students to choose any topic for their book covers and checks to make sure they are writing or drawing the information in appropriate places. The activity on page 203 works with this strategy. Model this strategy several times with the class. Then have students work with partners to design a book cover. Once students have had more experience locating the various parts of a book cover, then they can do this activity independently. (Standards 5.1, 5.2, 7.1, 8.5)

Determine Importance—
Using Parts of the Book

Strategy 6: Parts of the Book Checklist

The activity on page 204 is provided for this strategy. Students examine a nonfiction book that contains a table of contents, index, glossary, etc. A textbook works well for this activity. Students spend some time looking through their books and then check off the different items found in the book. Students should tell something about each item in the "Information" column. Provide plenty of time for students to look through their books to become familiar and comfortable with them. (Standards 5.2, 7.1, 7.3, 7.4)

Strategy 7: Inside or Outside?

Use the activity on page 205 for practice with this strategy. The teacher reads the directions with students and then reads through all of the words on the page. Next, students cut out the labels for different parts of a book. After students have finished cutting, they should sort the words into two categories: "Inside" and "Outside." The teacher discusses where each of the items is found in a book. Then students glue the words in the correct columns. If students think an item can belong in both categories, they should glue it in the middle. Before completing this activity, students should spend ample time looking through their textbooks to feel comfortable with them. Textbooks are a new experience for most young students, and they need help identifying the various parts of the book. This activity can also be done in small groups or with partners. (Standards 5.2, 5.6, 7.1)

Strategy 8: Locating Information

The activity on page 206 is helpful with this strategy. Students think about where they would find parts of a book such as the copyright page, table of contents, dedication, title page, introduction, appendix, bibliography, glossary, and index. This activity can be done as a whole class, in small groups, or individually—as a pre-assessment, post-assessment, or both. (Standard 5.2)

Strategy 9: Make an Index

For this strategy, students will create their own indexes using vocabulary words from a nonfiction book. A template on page 207 can be used with this strategy. On the lines provided, students write vocabulary words from the nonfiction book they are reading. They should only choose words that are important to the book's topic. Then students should write the page number where they found the word. Next, students cut out the words and rearrange them in alphabetical order. Finally, they glue them onto another sheet of paper. Now they have an index to go with their book. (Standards 5.2, 5.4, 5.6, 5.7, 7.1)

Strategy 10: Make Your Own Picture Glossary

The teacher can use glossaries with pictures to introduce students to the concept of glossaries. This strategy teaches students how to use pictures to locate words or topics in the glossary. Once they have had practice using this strategy, students (in small groups) choose five words from a nonfiction text being used in class. They then write the words in alphabetical order and create pictures that show the words' meanings. For guided practice, the teacher can use the template on page 208 to have students alphabetize and illustrate the words in glossary format. (Standards 5.1, 5.2, 5.4, 5.6, 7.1)

Determine Importance—
Using Parts of the Book

Table of Contents

Directions: Find the table of contents in your book. Look at the information and answer the following questions.

1. How is the table of contents organized?

   _____

2. How many pages are in your book?

   _____

3. How many chapters does your book have?

   _____

4. Using the table of contents, see if your book has any of the following. Write **yes** or **no** next to each book part.

   Glossary _____   Bibliography _____

   Appendix _____   Index _____

Write two questions you have about this book from the information you have learned in the table of contents.

1. _____

   _____

   _____

2. _____

   _____

   _____

Determine Importance— Using Parts of the Book

Create a Table of Contents

Directions: Using a nonfiction book, make a table of contents. Do not look at the existing table of contents, if there is one. Look through all of the chapters and make up your own.

Table of Contents

Chapter title / Section		Page number
_____	. . . .	_____
_____	. . . .	_____
_____	. . . .	_____
_____	. . . .	_____
_____	. . . .	_____
_____	. . . .	_____
_____	. . . .	_____
_____	. . . .	_____
_____	. . . .	_____
_____	. . . .	_____
_____	. . . .	_____
_____	. . . .	_____
_____	. . . .	_____
_____	. . . .	_____

Determine Importance—
Using Parts of the Book

Using the Newspaper

Directions: Find the table of contents of a newspaper. Locate the following sections and write the page number for each:

Section	Page
Weather	___
Movies	___
Sports	___
Comics	___

Write two other interesting facts you have learned about your newspaper from the table of contents:

1. _____

_____

_____

_____

2. _____

_____

_____

_____

Determine Importance—Using Parts of the Book

Asking Questions

Directions: Read the table of contents below. Write five questions about this table of contents. Make an answer key on a separate sheet of paper. Give your questions to your partner to answer.

Table of Contents

---

1. _____

    _____

2. _____

    _____

3. _____

    _____

4. _____

    _____

5. _____

    _____

Determine Importance—
Using Parts of the Book

Design a Book Cover

Directions: Design a cover for a nonfiction book. Remember to include:

- the title of the book
- the author's name
- the illustrator's name
- a picture

Determine Importance—
Using Parts of the Book

Parts of the Book Checklist

Directions: Check off the different items found in the book. Also write the page numbers where they are located. Include some of the information that you found for each book part.

Parts of the book	Yes	No	Page	Information
1. title				
2. author				
3. illustrator				
4. copyright				
5. publisher				
6. place of publication				
7. table of contents				
8. map				
9. chart				
10. caption				
11. appendix				
12. glossary				
13. index				
14. bibliography				

Determine Importance—Using Parts of the Book

Inside or Outside?

Directions: Cut out the different parts of a book listed below. Sort them into the two categories. Glue them in the correct columns. If you think an item belongs in both categories, glue it in the middle.

Outside the book	Inside the book

Copyright date	Chapter names
Table of contents	Bibliography
Title page	Index
Title of the book	Glossary
Author's name	Appendix
Cover of the book	Spine of the book

Determine Importance— Using Parts of the Book

Locating Information

Directions: Use the words in the word bank to answer the questions below.

copyright page	dedication	introduction
table of contents	title page	appendix
bibliography	glossary	index

Where would you look to find the following:

1. The year the book was published: _____

2. The place of publication: _____

3. Where the author thanks people: _____

4. The reason that the book was written: _____

5. A specific chapter: _____

6. The meaning of special words: _____

7. Where certain information is located in the book: _____

8. What books the author used to write his or her book:

   _____

9. A map or illustration: _____

Determine Importance—
Using Parts of the Book

Make an Index

Directions: On the lines below, write vocabulary words from the nonfiction book you are reading. Choose words that are important to the book's topic. Write the page number where you found the word. Cut out the strips and arrange them in alphabetical order. Glue them onto another sheet of paper. Now you have an index to go with your book.

_____	_____
_____	_____
_____	_____
_____	_____
_____	_____
_____	_____
_____	_____
_____	_____
_____	_____

Determine Importance—
Using Parts of the Book

Make Your Own Picture Glossary

Directions: Choose five important words from a nonfiction book that relate to the main idea. Put them in alphabetical order below and then illustrate.

1. _____

2. _____

3. _____

4. _____

5. _____

PASSPORT TO COMPREHENSION

Visualize

Visualize

Visualizing encompasses all the senses—seeing, hearing, tasting, touching, and smelling. Through visualizing the information or events presented in the text, students are able to picture the facts and details in a multidimensional fashion. Visualizing the information increases the chances that students will retain and recall the information at a later time. When students create images, they can add important details to the facts and information presented in the text. Student can visualize what the object might smell like, feel like, taste like, sound like, or look like. These sensory images make the text come alive, make the reading more enjoyable, and increase students' interest and motivation in reading more of the text (Harvey 1998).

Some researchers believe that students' abilities to visualize are closely connected to their abilities to think. Thinking is linked to the ability to make abstract thoughts concrete, and students' abilities to visualize are part of this process. Research demonstrates that students with strong reading skills automatically and instinctively construct pictures in their minds. In other words, students actually see what is being read.

Visualization is a skill that can be taught to most students. Through direct instruction, the teacher can show students how to use and apply visualization skills to assist in understanding the information. Over time, as students' reading abilities improve, they will have an easier time visualizing the information, sequence of events, and directions, and will incorporate this knowledge into their own personal banks of information. Students can use visualization skills to create mental pictures of the facts and details not mentioned in the text (Cunningham and Allington 1999). There are many ways of introducing this type of reading strategy to students.

When visualizing, students bring their prior knowledge and experiences on the topic and meld it with the new information from the text. Students use these experiences to create new and unique mental images when reading nonfiction texts. As they read and then listen to classmates sharing information and interpretations, students adjust visual images to reflect the new information. They also incorporate the new information with prior information, knowledge, and experiences to create unique images about the situation, setting, events, people, etc. These images connect students personally, and sometimes permanently, with the text.

When students visualize, they are creating a "movie" in their head. Students' visual creations are unique. No other student will "see" the information in the exact same way. Through visualizing, students develop the characters, create the setting, personalize the information, stay engaged in the text, and are eager to read to learn more about the topic (Harvey and Goudvis 2000). It is often difficult to see a movie based on a book after the book has been read. The characters, settings, and events in the movie never measure up to the visual images that students (readers) create in their minds.

Visualize

Research shows that students who are proficient readers purposefully and strategically create visual images during and after reading nonfiction texts. This visualization allows students to monitor their understanding of the text and to adjust their reading strategy accordingly if comprehension begins to falter. When creating visual images, students involve their emotions and senses. These emotions and sensory images connect the new information to the students' prior knowledge on the topic. Students who are proficient readers understand the role that visualizing plays in enhancing their comprehension of the information (Keene and Zimmermann 1997). Visualizing text allows students to take words from the text and form images that are real and concrete. This process enhances students' comprehension of the text (Harvey and Goudvis 2000). A teacher can teach students to construct visual images by having them read (or listen to) a part of a text, by having them stop to think about and reflect upon the text, and by having them visualize the text's information (Harvey and Goudvis 2000).

Students who read well use the visual images they have created to immerse themselves in the details of the text. The text's details give the words dimension and meaning, grab students' attention, and make the text more memorable to them (Keene and Zimmermann 1997).

Here are some other easy ways to have students practice using visualization skills:

- The teacher reads 3–4 pages of the text aloud to students. Both the teacher and students share the visual images that they created in their minds.

- The teacher reads a picture book aloud without showing the illustrations to students. The teacher encourages students to share what they are "seeing" and compare their drawings to the actual illustrations in the text.

- The teacher has students sketch pictures or diagrams that represents what they "see" in their minds and then share their sketches with the teacher and the class.

Visualizing is linked to metacognition. Metacognition is the awareness of what we are thinking. The importance of visualization extends beyond enhancing one's understanding and recall of information. Visualization also requires students to practice reflecting upon their thinking and how it relates to their own personal knowledge. Visualization enables students to integrate this new information with their prior knowledge and experiences on the topic. This integration is a key factor in good comprehension.

According to Harvey and Goudvis (2000), visualization and interpretation are closely linked, and together these two reading strategies enhance students' comprehension of the text. The act of visualizing the facts and details strengthens students' interpretation skills. When students visualize information, they are also interpreting the information. Instead of seeing words, students are seeing mental images (Harvey and Goudvis 2000).

Visualize

Students with strong reading skills automatically create mental images while reading. The visual images and interpretations that students create are unique to each student (Rasinski and Padak 2000). Students who are proficient readers use the visual images to draw conclusions, develop unique interpretations of the text's information, recall the facts and details presented in the text, and recall the information after the text has been read. As the text is being read, the teacher reminds students to create images in their minds about the information. After the text has been read, the teacher has students draw pictures representing the content of the reading. Then the students share their drawings.

Good readers know that creating visual images increases their understanding of important facts and details, enables them to retain and to connect the new information to prior knowledge and experiences, and enables them to target inconsistent statements between different paragraphs of the text. Another outcome of visualizing the information is that students must first organize it in a logical manner in their minds. Students can share this information with other classmates during group discussions, or "retrieve" this information when answering a question.

Strategy 1: Image in My Mind

The teacher models how to create an image out of the information in his or her mind. This image helps the teacher (or student) understand the information from the text and link it to any prior information or experiences. (Standards 5.1, 5.2, 7.1, 7.2, 7.4)

Strategy 2: Creating a "Movie"

Working with small groups, the teacher has students draw a representation of the visual images they created. Model this strategy with the whole class several times before having them try it. The picture does not have to be a "work of art," but should capture the essence of the most important facts or details from the text, according to each student. The teacher collects the drawings made by each student in the group. The template on page 221 can be used for this strategy. (Standards 5.1, 7.1, 7.2)

Strategy 3: Seeing Color and Shape

The teacher shows students a variety of colored geometric shapes. (Pattern blocks, wooden beads, wooden blocks, etc., are ideal for this activity.) The teacher selects one shape and has students closely examine the shape. The teacher hides the shape and asks students to close their eyes and visualize what the shape looked like—its size, form, color, weight, etc. Students draw pictures of the shape, including all of the details they see in their "mind's eye." The activity on page 222 can be used for this strategy. (Standards 5.1, 7.4)

Visualize

Strategy 4: Visualizing Concrete Objects Using the Senses

The teacher shows students an object. The object can be a box of crayons, a piece of sporting equipment, a teddy bear, a bouquet or a single flower, etc. The teacher encourages students to involve all of their senses when they examine the object. Students can smell it, touch it, see it, shake it (if appropriate for the item), or taste it (if appropriate for the item). The teacher then has students describe the object to a classmate, including all of the details about the object that they can remember. The activity on page 223 can be used for this strategy. (Standards 5.1, 7.4, 8.5)

Strategy 5: Visualizing Distant Objects

The teacher has students visualize an object that can be found in their homes. Have students share the visual images with a classmate. Make sure they include as much detail about the object as possible, such as:

- the color of the object
- the size and weight of the object
- how the object looks and feels
- what it tastes like (if appropriate)
- what it smells like (if appropriate)
- what it sounds like (if appropriate)

The activity on page 224 can be used for this strategy. To extend this activity, the teacher can have students draw a picture of what they are visualizing or have the classmate who listened to the description of the object draw a picture to represent what they understand the object to be. The classmate can share the picture with the student who provided the description. The student can see at a glance how accurate his or her description of the item was and realize what important details need to be included when describing an object to another person. (Standards 5.1, 7.4, 8.5)

Strategy 6: Listening to Narrative

The teacher reads a short selection from a text. Students listen to the text while keeping their eyes closed. After reading, the teacher has students describe the visual images they created. As a follow-up activity, the teacher can have students draw a picture of the images. The teacher can model this by reading a piece of text aloud and then drawing what comes to mind for students to see. Students can discuss if they saw the same images. (Standards 5.1, 7.4, 8.5)

STRATEGIES AND SKILLS
PASSPORT TO COMPREHENSION

Visualize

Strategy 7: Visualizing During and After Reading

While reading or listening to the text, the teacher encourages students to form images of the information in their minds. By doing this, students are keeping focused on the information being shared in the text and are using visual images to enhance their understanding of the information. The activity on page 225 can be used for this strategy. (Standards 5.1, 7.1)

Strategy 8: Visualizing Important Facts and Details

When using this strategy, the teacher has students respond to the text in a way that will help them visualize or imagine the information. The teacher can have students draw something that was not pictured in the text or draw something that requires them to respond to the text in a more personal manner (Cunningham and Allington 1999). To extend this strategy, students can write a brief response about the drawing and how the drawing helped them understand the information from the text. Use the activity on page 226 for this strategy. (Standards 5.1, 7.4, 8.5)

Strategy 9: Sketch to Stretch

Sketch to stretch is a nonverbal response activity that can be used during and after reading in order to extend students' comprehension of the text and develop their visualization skills. Sketch to Stretch has students draw visual images (either during or after reading the text) of a memorable or important event from the text on a piece of paper. The teacher can use students' drawings as the foundation for interpretive discussion about the text (Rasinski and Padak 2000). The result is that all students participate in a discussion using higher-level thinking skills (Rasinski and Padak 2000).

Students share their drawings with their classmates in a small-group setting. Instead of having students describe their drawings, the classmates share their own interpretations of the drawings. Classmates might ask students questions such as "What is this picture about?" "Why did the illustrator think this was an important event?" "What do you think this picture means and why?" After the classmates share their opinions, students can explain their drawings and the significance of them. (Standards 5.1, 7.2, 8.5)

Strategy 10: Listening Center—Comparing Pictures

Teachers can set up a listening center filled with illustrated books on tape. Students listen to the tape two times before they even see the book's cover. Then they read the book, either with the tape's support or independently, and fill out "Comparing Pictures" on page 227. (Standards 5.1, 7.4)

Visualize

Strategy 11: Group Mapping

Group mapping is a way to promote students' responses to reading and build a framework for discussing the text. After reading the text, students can develop maps showing the important concepts presented in the text. The drawings do not have to be works of art; instead, they represent what students learned and understand from the text. The completed maps are then shared with classmates. Classmates may ask questions or make comments about the maps. As a result of the questions and comments, discussion of the text is fostered and learning is extended (Rasinski and Padak 2000). Model this strategy several times with the class before having them try it. (Standards 5.1, 5.2)

Strategy 12: What's Missing?

During infancy, humans develop constancy—they begin to fill in what's missing from their lines of sight. That's why peek-a-boo doesn't delight a two-year-old; the tot figured out long ago that your face was still there behind your hands, even though it wasn't visible. You can build on this foundation by showing students cutaway diagrams and asking them to visualize and draw the missing portion. For example, take an 8" x 10" illustration and cover two sections of it with sticky notes and photocopy it. Then have students try to draw in the "missing" information. Use the activity on page 228 for practice with this strategy. (Standards 5.1, 5.2)

Strategy 13: Visualizing Missing Details

Using clues from the illustrations, skillful readers visualize the missing pictures that link the illustrations together and allow the story to make sense. Thus, it's beneficial to use wordless picture books to teach the strategy of visualizing missing details (Rose 1991). Go through a wordless picture book with the class, looking at and discussing the pictures. Ask students to draw what they visualize happening between two of the pictures and write one sentence to explain their picture. For example, in the book *Carl's Afternoon in the Park* by Alexandra Day, there is a picture of a rottweiler puppy at the top of a slide and a toddler standing at the bottom. The next illustration shows the puppy on top of the toddler, who is sprawled on the ground at the base of the slide. Students will enjoy drawing the missing event of the puppy going down the slide, and your quick scan of each student's drawing will enable you to immediately detect misconceptions so that you can address such problems quickly. You can find other good examples in any of the Carl books by Alexandra Day or the book *Tuesday* by David Weisner. The activity on page 229 provides more practice. (Standards 5.1, 5.2)

Strategy 14: Pictures in the Mind

To ensure that students know what you mean by "pictures in the mind," have them do this simple but effective activity. Have each student fold a large sheet of white construction paper into sixths. Say, "Close your eyes. You see yellow—nothing but the color yellow. It's as if you are being swallowed up by the color yellow. Now the yellow is changing into a shape; it's turning into something—what is it? Don't answer out loud; you'll be able to draw it and share it with the class in a minute. Instead, notice the details of your object. The more detailed your drawing, the better. Open your eyes and draw your item in the first box." Repeat this procedure each day using a different color. (Standards 5.1, 5.2)

Visualize

Strategy 15: Text Response Centers

Rotate students through these five text response centers to create lasting impressions of text (Keene and Zimmerman 1997).

Models—At the Models Center, students can create three-dimensional representations of their favorite images from a text. Provide pipe cleaners, plenty of tagboard, modeling clay in many colors, tape, glue sticks, scissors, cotton balls, and craft sticks at this center.

Studio—In the Studio, students create an artistic response to text. Provide different sizes and colors of unlined paper, crayons, colored pencils, markers, glue sticks, fabric scraps, string, scissors, watercolor paints, and brushes. Students can make a frame for their artwork with construction paper. Students can tape a sheet of lined paper to the bottom of the frame to allow viewers to react to their creations. Students can display their responses in the room or the hall. Expect unusual and vivid responses. Occasionally ask students to describe their work to the class, explaining why they selected particular media and colors to express their ideas.

Drama—At the Drama Center, students can act out the events they have read about. An easy way is to provide students with crayons, markers, yarn, fabric scraps, sequins, buttons, staples and a stapler, glue, scissors, empty paper towel tubes (cut in half) or toilet paper tubes, and lots of photocopies of the puppet patterns on page 230. One child can manage two such puppets (one on each forefinger). A stage can be constructed out of a large, empty cardboard box. (Appliance boxes are especially good.) Cut away the sides of the box until just three attached sides remain. Using the existing folds of the box, bend the sides so that they flare out to provide the puppeteers with elbow room. Cut out a window in the front of the box in one of two ways: cut out a large window area and drape a cloth behind it, which the children move aside when performing, or leave the "shutters" on so you can "close the curtain" by shutting them. If you leave the shutters on, you will need to use Velcro® on the back sides of the shutters and the front of the theater to keep the shutters from closing during the performances.

Writer's Nook—At the Writer's Nook, students write about a favorite or strong image generated while reading the text. This station needs lined paper, a stapler and staples, pencils or pens of different colors, construction paper, glue, and scissors. Students can create a construction-paper frame around their written work and display it for others to read. They can also tape a lined sheet of paper to the bottom of the frame to give readers an opportunity to write a reaction to their writing.

Text Club—The purpose of the Text Club is to get together and discuss what's been read. To create a relaxed atmosphere conducive to conversation, this center needs comfortable chairs or carpet squares, pretzels or oyster crackers, and cups of water. Stress to students that they are to discuss their favorite images from the text. Because nothing concrete is produced in this center, tape record these discussions to keep students on track. Spot-check these discussions to be sure the students are staying focused.

Talk about student work from each center. Then students know that you value what they have produced, and you have an opportunity to show the rest of the class what you want to see produced at each center. For example, you can read aloud a child's response from the Writer's Nook and say, "I liked how Jill used red ink to write her response to the passage we read about volcanoes. It helps me to sense the intense heat given off by volcanic smoke, ash, and lava." (Standards 5.1, 7.2, 7.3, 7.4, 8.5)

Visualize

Strategy 16: Visual Presentations

An effective way to help students bridge the gap between imagination and text is to have them turn written material into visual presentations. You can accomplish this task by asking students to conduct research and figure out a visual way to show what they've learned. This method causes students to process information deeply while simultaneously preventing plagiarism. Students can portray the information in a diagram, flow chart, graph, chart, drawing, or computer multimedia presentation. For example, after students have read an expository piece in which a sequence of steps or events is described, have them express the information in a flow chart, either by hand or with the use of computer software. Challenge them by saying that they are trying to explain the process to kindergartners (who can't read anything more than the most basic of words, if that) and so their process must be explained visually with arrows between the steps. You may be amazed at how your students who struggle to express themselves in speech or in writing excel at this project. (Standards 5.1, 7.1, 7.2, 7.3, 7.4)

Some good topics for this kind of activity include the following:

- Where does garbage go after the trash collectors pick it up?
- How is sewage treated?
- How is water treated (purified)?
- Describe an animal's life cycle.
- Illustrate the water cycle.

Strategy 17: Examining Art with the Senses

Gather copies of art masterpieces and impressionistic art for this activity. Show students a piece of artwork. Do a think-aloud in which you discuss what the artwork evokes in your senses of sound, touch, taste, and smell. Explain thoroughly why the masterpiece affects you this way. For example, here's a sample think-aloud for Mary Cassatt's painting of a mother washing her daughter's feet in a basin of water: "I hear the splashing as the mother gently moves her hands over the child's feet and her voice as she murmurs loving words to her daughter. I feel the cool water and the warm weight of the child on her mother's lap. I smell the child's warm skin and the mother's perfume—lilac—I think. I do not get an image of taste from this picture. Not all images can create a response for every sense." Then, using a different piece of artwork, ask students to record what the piece evokes in their senses of sound, touch, taste, and smell. Discuss why they think it affects them in that way. (Standards 5.1, 5.2, 5.6, 8.5)

Strategy 18: 3-D

Help students visualize maps by creating a three-dimensional town on cardboard, graph paper, or a large piece of cloth with a checkered pattern. They can use blocks, blue ribbons (for streams and rivers), drinking straws and toothpicks (for bridges and railroad tracks). Ask them to label the street names with adhesive stickers and then have them drive miniature cars on a specified route. (Standards 5.1, 5.2, 7.1, 7.2, 7.3)

Visualize

Strategy 19: Quick Sketch

You can use the quick sketch technique to prompt students to visualize written material while simultaneously giving you the opportunity to monitor their visualizations (Rose 1991). Stop reading at the end of each paragraph of text and have students quickly (in 30–40 seconds) sketch what they've seen. Since these sketches should be made rapidly and without elaboration, provide students with crayons, oil pastels, or washable markers. These materials will encourage speed so that the lesson can keep moving forward. If students balk at creating images quickly and without much detail, explain that these drawings are just basic outlines to remind them of the vivid, detailed pictures they've created in their minds. (Standards 5.1, 8.2)

Strategy 20: Using Prior Knowledge

Hand out a large piece of unlined, white drawing paper to students and have them draw what they know about a subject before reading about it. For example, if you are going to learn about reading an analog clock face in math class, cover all the analog clocks in the room; then ask students to draw what they think a clock face looks like.

Prereading Drawing

Postreading Drawing

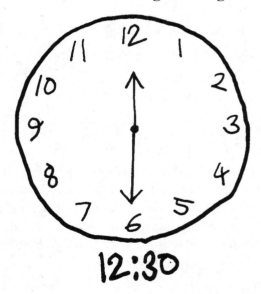

You can see that this student revised his or her mental image to include the correct number of hours on a clock face, the difference in the length of the clock hands, and the proper way to write a time. This activity is powerful proof of what each student learned and provides a good portfolio piece. (Standards 5.1, 5.2, 7.1, 7.4)

Visualize

Strategy 21: Sensory Collages

This activity is easiest to use with fiction texts. Have students respond to literature by creating collages of hand-drawn pictures and pictures cut from old magazines. Ask them to include at least one picture for each sense. They should have a picture that shows something they saw during the reading as well as one for:

- what they heard
- what they tasted
- what they felt (emotion)
- what they smelled
- what they touched

(Standards 5.1, 5.2, 7.4)

Strategy 22: Sensory Imaging Graphic Organizer

Introduce the Sensory Imaging Graphic Organizer on page 231 by analyzing ordinary objects that students encounter in their daily lives. Ask students to identify the elements of the objects that affect each of their senses and fill in the graphic organizer. Model this activity by showing students a pie pan and doing a think-aloud to complete the graphic organizer. Explain that although the pie pan has no food in it, it evokes these memories for you. After students have had some experience with this, bring in items related to an upcoming nonfiction passage and have students fill in the graphic organizers before reading (if they have any prior knowledge of the subject) or after reading (if they don't have prior knowledge of the subject). (Standards 5.1, 7.4)

Item	Looks	Feels	Smells	Sounds	Tastes
pie pan	round, large, ceramic	heavy, breakable	like my Grandma's kitchen	like lots of people talking around a table	like apple pie a la mode

Strategy 23: Using Emotions

Some of the longest-lasting images come from the emotions rather than the senses. An important strategy to help students connect emotionally with text is to read a passage about the same event written from two different points of view. Considering different viewpoints will give students a well-rounded understanding of the situation. For example, if you are reading about life on the African savannah and how lions chase and eat gazelles, read one version from the perspective of a lion and the other from the perspective of a gazelle. Then ask questions such as:

- What emotions did you feel as a lion?
- What did you think when you saw the herd of grazing gazelles?
- How did you feel toward the gazelles?
- What emotions did you feel as a gazelle?
- What was your first thought when you noticed the lion sneaking through the tall grass?
- How did you feel toward the lions?

(Standards 7.1, 7.2, 7.4, 8.2)

Visualize

Creating a "Movie"

Directions: What did you see after reading (or listening to) the text? Draw a picture showing what you visualized.

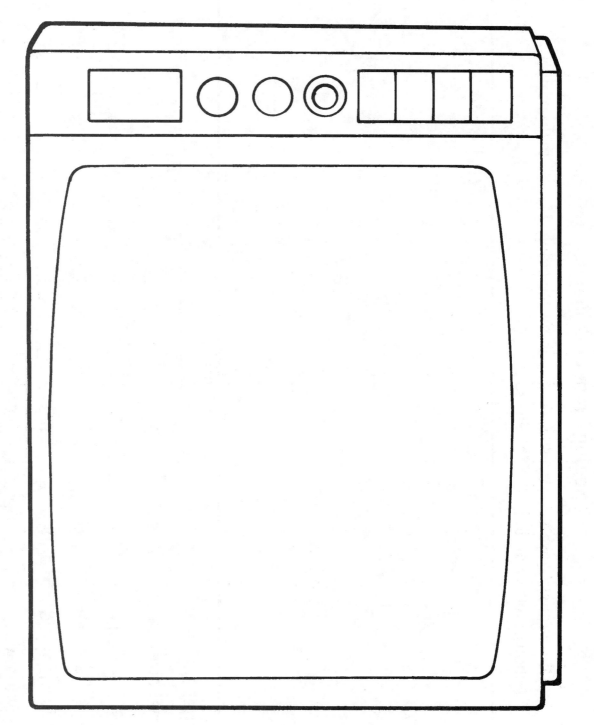

Visualize

Seeing Color and Shape

Directions: Close your eyes and think about the colored shape that you were shown. Draw a picture of the shape.

1. What shape did you see? _____

2. What size was the shape? _____

3. What color was the shape? _____

4. Was the shape heavy or light? _____

5. How many sides did the shape have? _____

6. How many corners did the shape have? _____

7. What else do you remember about the shape? _____

Visualize

Visualizing Concrete Objects Using the Senses

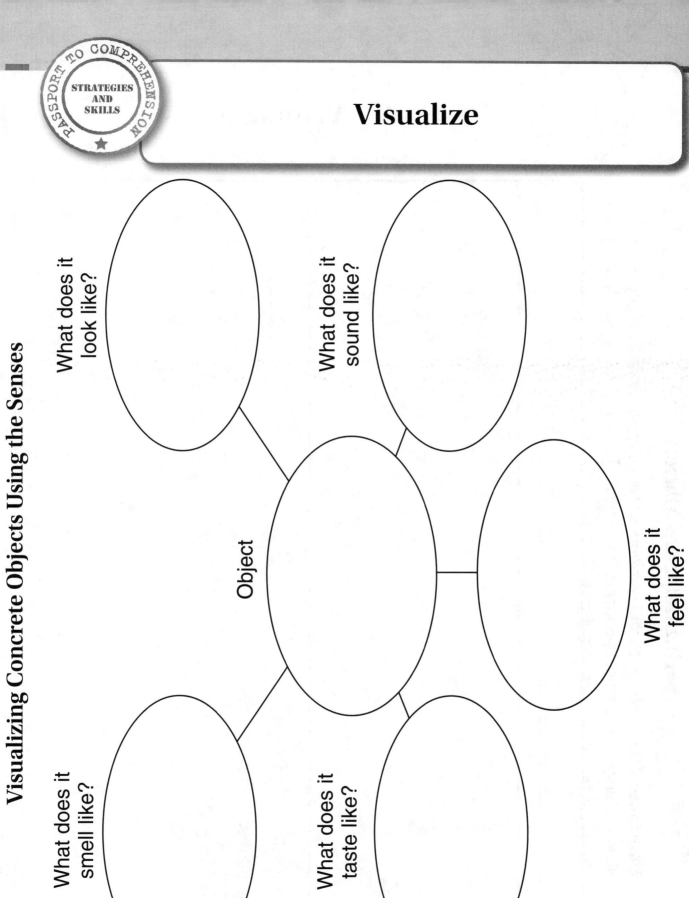

What does it look like?

What does it sound like?

Object

What does it feel like?

What does it smell like?

What does it taste like?

Visualize

Visualizing Distant Objects

Directions: Think of an object from home, from the playground, from a favorite place to visit, etc. Draw a picture of the object. In your drawing, include as many details as possible about the object.

Object: _____

Visualize

Visualizing During and After Reading

Title of text: _____

After reading, I visualized _____

During reading, I visualized _____

Visualize

Visualizing Important Facts and Details

Directions: Draw what you think is important in the text. Write a sentence telling why you think this image is important.

Title of text: _____

This is a picture of: _____

This drawing helps me understand the text by: _____

Visualize

Comparing Pictures

Directions: Answer the questions below.

1. How were the book's pictures **like** the ones you saw in your mind? Tell at least two ways that they were alike.

_____

_____

_____

2. How were the book's pictures **different** from the ones you saw in your mind? Tell at least two ways that they were different.

_____

_____

_____

3. Which pictures did you like better?

_____

_____

_____

4. Why? Give at least two reasons.

_____

_____

_____

Visualize

What's Missing?

Directions: Complete the picture. Then, on the back of this paper, draw what the dollhouse looks like from the front.

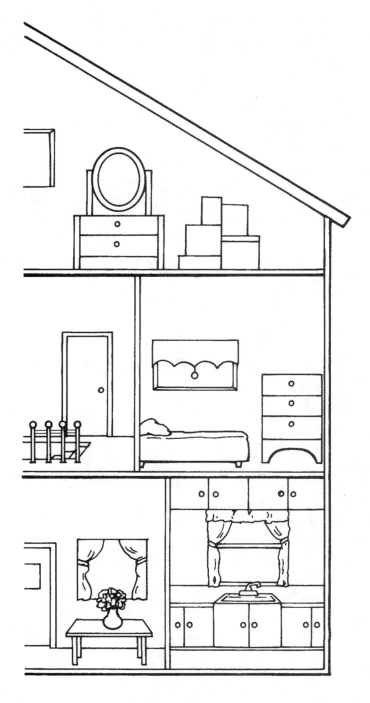

Visualize

Visualizing Missing Details

Directions: Look at the illustrations. Think about what is happening in each story. Then draw in the missing pictures to complete each story.

Visualize

Puppet Patterns for Drama Center

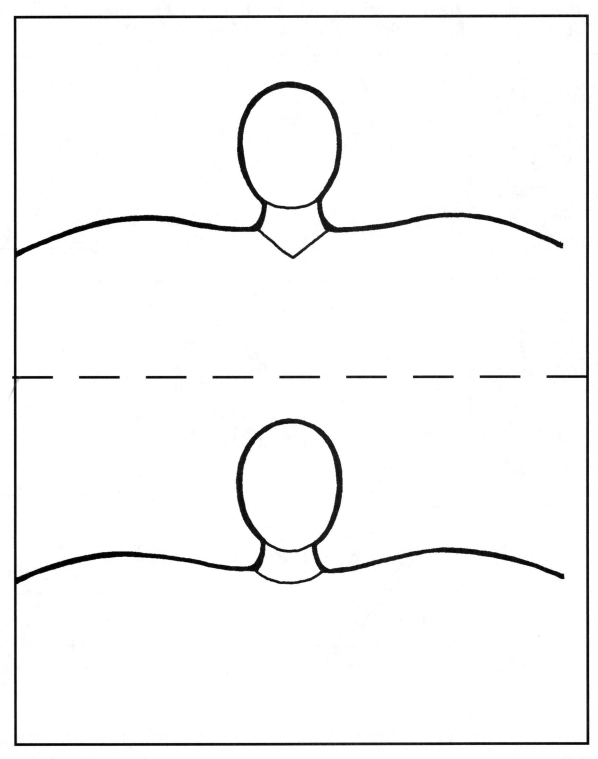

Visualize

Sensory Imaging Graphic Organizer

Directions: Choose some items from your home or classroom. In the boxes below, list the item and tell how it affects each of your five senses.

Item	Looks	Feels	Smells	Sounds	Tastes

Notes

Summarize and Synthesize

PASSPORT TO COMPREHENSION

Summarize and Synthesize

As students are learning to read and comprehend nonfiction texts, teachers need to evaluate students' understandings. Students' responses to text inform teachers if students are engaged and understanding the material. One skill students need to be taught is how to summarize. Reading a text, deciding on the important ideas in the text, and putting them together in one's own words is summarizing. Summarizing requires students to be able to select only what is important from a text. Reading for understanding and summarizing text are higher-level thinking skills. Summarizing also sets a purpose for reading, actively involving students while they read. Paraphrasing is the process of restating, in one's own words, what was read. Paraphrasing is a way for students to tell the main ideas of a text in their own words, thereby making the text easier to understand for other students. Synthesizing requires students to take new information, compare it to what they already know, and make speculations or draw conclusions.

Summarizing can be taught through direct instruction. The teacher must model for students how to find, understand, and organize information from nonfiction texts. Prior to modeling strategies, the teacher sets guidelines for summarizing and paraphrasing. A chart outlining these guidelines can be displayed as a visual reminder of the process. The guidelines for summarizing might be the following:

1. Read the text.
2. Reread the text, looking for important information and main ideas.
3. Decide which information is important.
4. Record the information in a graphic organizer.
5. Use the information to write a short summary in a way that makes sense.
6. Only tell what is important.

The following strategies can be taught during shared reading, guided reading, and mini-lessons. Teachers can use whole- or small-group instruction.

Strategy 1: Time Line

A time line is a chart that helps students understand what happened in a text and when it happened. Information is organized in a linear fashion. The events are labeled and written in the order in which they happened. A time line works well with different types of expository text. In science, the life cycles of animals or information about plant growth can be presented in a linear chart. After the text is read, the students and teacher can work together to sequence the events. Use the template for a time line on page 241. See the example below. (Standards 5.1, 5.2, 7.2, 7.3, 7.4)

Topic: Life Cycle of a Frog

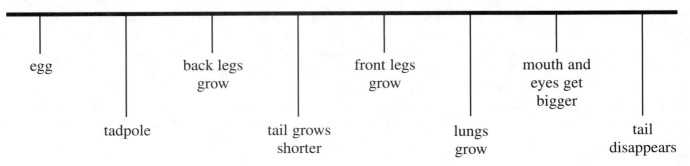

Summarize and Synthesize

Strategy 2: Data Chart

A data chart is a good graphic organizer to use when comparing information about two animals, people, plants, etc. It is a simple three-column chart with the categories being compared listed vertically in the middle column, and two columns for the things being compared. If the book is about how Pilgrims lived, the students would compare the Pilgrims to themselves. They would need to gather information from the text to fill in the column about Pilgrims. The chart might look like the following:

Pilgrims		Us
	Clothes	
	Jobs	
	School	
	Food	
	Home	

A template for a data chart is on page 242. Teachers can fill in the categories and topics for students before copying. (Standards 5.2, 7.1, 7.2, 7.3, 7.4)

Strategy 3: Topic Web

Webs are wonderful tools that can be used to teach various types of comprehension. They are often used with students because they are one of the easiest ways to display information. The teacher helps students locate the main idea of the text, which is then written in the center oval. In the ovals around the main idea, students record important information. This web allows students to summarize the important information. Then the information can be paraphrased by writing about the web and drawing a picture. A blank topic web is provided on page 243. (Standards 5.1, 5.2, 7.2, 7.3)

Strategy 4: Nonfiction Story Map

Students often use story maps to help describe the important characters and events from fiction stories. Story maps can also help students organize information from a nonfiction story. You can use story maps in a variety of ways. Prior to using the activity on page 244, introduce nonfiction story maps by giving students a large, blank piece of white paper. Students can work in guided-reading groups, as a class, with a partner, or independently. Have students read a short nonfiction text selection. Then they write the topic at the top of the page. Next, discuss the most important facts from the story. Students draw illustrations of these facts and label each one with one sentence. Finally, students use their story maps to give a summary of their reading to a classmate. After students have done this activity several times, give them the activity to complete on their own as a follow-up to reading a nonfiction selection. (Standards 5.1, 5.2, 7.2, 7.3)

Summarize and Synthesize

Strategy 5: Summary Cards

Using summary cards to record and organize important information is an introduction to paragraph writing that is appropriate for young students. Before a text is read aloud, the teacher instructs students to be "detail detectives." They will signal the teacher with a thumbs up when they hear important information. The teacher will stop reading to record a few words of the important information on a card. As the information is recorded, the cards are put in a chart. When students first begin this activity, they may think everything is important. The teacher does not question their suggestions at this time. They are all written down. After the book has been read, the teacher reads over the information collected on the cards. Together the teacher and students begin to sort the cards. First, students sort the cards into important details and unimportant details. Then the important details are sorted into categories (food, shelter, etc.) or in an order that makes sense. The cards are read as a summary once they have been ordered. Students can make their own cards, cut them out, and glue them, in order, on another piece of paper during a guided-reading lesson. The cards should include illustrations. A blank template for summary cards is provided on page 245. (Standards 7.2, 7.3, 8.2, 8.5)

Strategy 6: Compare and Summarize

Teachers use many different graphic organizers to help compare information from expository texts. The Compare and Summarize sheet on page 246 is a simple comparison chart. Students list the two items they will compare, and then under each item, list examples that state how they are similar. For example, students write *frogs* at the top of one column and *toads* at the top of the other. Then they go through their book and write details that are the same about frogs and toads. After they have included all the samples from the text, they reread their information and either paraphrase it or write a one-sentence summary about how frogs and toads are similar. (Standards 5.1, 5.2, 7.1, 7.2, 7.3)

Strategy 7: Compare and Contrast

The Compare and Contrast chart on page 247 is a simple diagram used to teach students how to compare and contrast two things. At the top, students fill in the two things they are comparing. Then they find details from the text that explain how they are alike and write them in one column. In the second column, they write how the two things are different. Using the first example, students write *frogs* and *toads* as the topics and then use the text to find examples of their similarities, listing these in the "Alike" column. Then they find examples of differences and list them in the "Different" column. After completing the top, they reread the information they have written on the chart and write a one- or two-sentence summary about how frogs and toads are both alike and different. (Standards 5.1, 5.2, 7.1, 7.2, 7.3)

Summarize and Synthesize

Strategy 8: Venn Diagram and Summary

Venn diagrams can help children compare two things that have some similarities and some differences. After filling in the Venn diagrams, students can use them to write short summaries. The blank Venn diagram on page 248 can be helpful for this strategy. (Standards 5.1, 5.2, 7.1, 7.2, 7.3, 7.4)

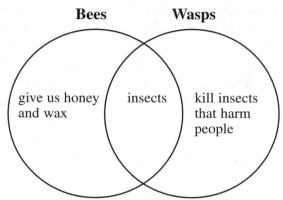

Summary: Both bees and wasps are insects that are useful to humans.

Strategy 9: Feature Analysis Diagram

Another way to compare and contrast characteristics of a concept is by using feature analysis. Begin by selecting a category that has two or more items that are similar. Then write these items, or examples, along the left side of the chart or board. Use a small amount of items. Across the top, write the features you will use to describe the items on the left. Go through the chart together, filling in whether the items possess each feature. Use a plus (+) for yes and a minus (−) for no. Finally, investigate the diagram as a class and discuss what you have discovered. The teacher may want to ask students questions about the diagram. At the end, write a summary statement of the class findings. If the class appears to be capable of summarizing information from graphic organizers, have students write their own summary statements after completing the chart. Use the Feature Analysis Diagram on page 249. The teacher will fill in examples on the left side of the diagram and features across the top of the diagram. (Standards 5.1, 5.2, 7.1, 7.2, 7.3, 7.4, 8.2)

Category: Animals

	backbone	lay eggs	warm-blooded	cold-blooded
fish	+	+	−	+
birds	+	+	+	−
mammals	+	−	+	−
reptiles	+	+	−	+

Summary: All types of animals compared on our chart have backbones, and most lay eggs.

Summarize and Synthesize

Strategy 10: Categorization Chart

Expository texts contain a wealth of information. It can be difficult for students to organize many different types of information in the same text. Nonfiction books often have more than one idea. Using a simple chart for categories helps organize information about different aspects of a topic. The teacher can write a short paragraph on chart paper to read with students. The teacher can then read through it again and construct a chart to fill in. The chart should be created during the lesson so students can see the thinking that accompanies reading. The paragraph should already be written. If the paragraph were about the sky at night, the chart might look like the following:

Stars	Moon	Planets	Comets
twinkle some are very bright	brightest light covered with craters	shine	shoot across sky have tails

After the reading is finished and the chart is filled in, the teacher and students review the chart and discuss which facts go together. A blank Categorization Chart is provided on page 250. The teacher can fill in the categories before copying the chart for students. (Standards 5.2, 7.1, 7.2, 7.3, 8.2, 8.5)

Strategy 11: Partner Reading

Partner reading requires careful preparation by the teacher. First, the teacher needs to think about who should partner with whom. Struggling readers should be paired with students who are able to help without just telling all of the words. The teacher should partner students who work well together. It may take some adjustments to have partnerships work well. Once they are formed, they can stay together for awhile. The teacher makes sure that the partners know how they will read; taking turns with each student reading a page is one way. The teacher must also remember to set a purpose for reading. When teaching students to focus on important information and how to summarize it, teachers must pose a question before the pairs begin to read. Now they have a purpose for reading. As the pairs read, they take notes. Each partner writes down at least one important fact. After reading, the pairs share their facts. Each pair can then write a short summary of what they learned and illustrate it. These can be combined into a class book. A blank organizer for partners to use is provided on page 251. (Standards 7.2, 7.3, 8.5)

Summarize and Synthesize

Strategy 12: Is It Important?

As students read, have them make two lists: one with important facts and one with unimportant facts. After completing their lists, they circle one fact on each list. At the bottom of the page, they justify why each fact belonged in that category. (Standards 7.2, 7.3, 7.4)

Strategy 13: Tell Me the Facts

After students practice categorizing important and unimportant facts by writing them, they will begin to do this as they read texts. They will eventually be able to go through texts and find only the important details. Have them use the activity on page 252 to write important facts in separate boxes. They can finish the activity by reading their summaries to a classmate or parent helper. (Standards 5.2, 7.1, 7.2, 7.3, 8.5)

Strategy 14: Summarize with the 5 Ws

The activity on page 253 teaches students to use the 5 Ws (who, what where, when, and why) to put together a written summary of a text. After filling in information for each of the 5 Ws, students should use this information to write a summary based on their title or topic. (Standards 7.2, 7.3, 8.2)

Strategy 15: Put It in Your Own Words

During guided reading, have students read a nonfiction book, or a short selection, if appropriate. Have them share with a partner (or a small group) what the book is about. After discussing the book, have students write what they think are the most important details or facts from the book. After finding the details, they can also rewrite the main idea in their own words, or make an illustration of their details. Presenting an oral summary to the class can vary this activity. Use the activities on pages 254 and 255 for practice with this strategy. (Standards 7.2, 7.3, 8.5)

Strategy 16: Bookmarks

Bookmarks help students stay focused on the purpose for reading as they work through a text during guided reading. They provide a place where students can write their thoughts as they read. Students cut blank bookmarks from a piece of paper. A prompt is written on one side of the bookmark to guide students in their reading. Bookmarks for expository text might have the following prompts:

- This is the main idea.
- This is an important detail.

As students read through the book, the answer to each prompt is written on the other side of the bookmark and put into the appropriate place in the book. The bookmarks can be used after reading to complete a graphic organizer and give oral summaries during class discussions. The teacher should limit the number of bookmarks students have. (Standards 7.2, 7.3)

Summarize and Synthesize

Time Line

Directions: Fill in the events from the text in the order in which they happened. In the numbered boxes, draw a picture for each event.

Title or topic: _____

1.	4.
2.	5.
3.	6.

Summarize and Synthesize

Data Chart

Directions: Use the chart to compare two items.

Book title or topic: _____

Item 1: _____   Item 2: _____

© Shell Education

Summarize and Synthesize

Topic Web

Directions: Write the main idea of your topic in the center oval. Write important information about the topic in the ovals connected to the center.

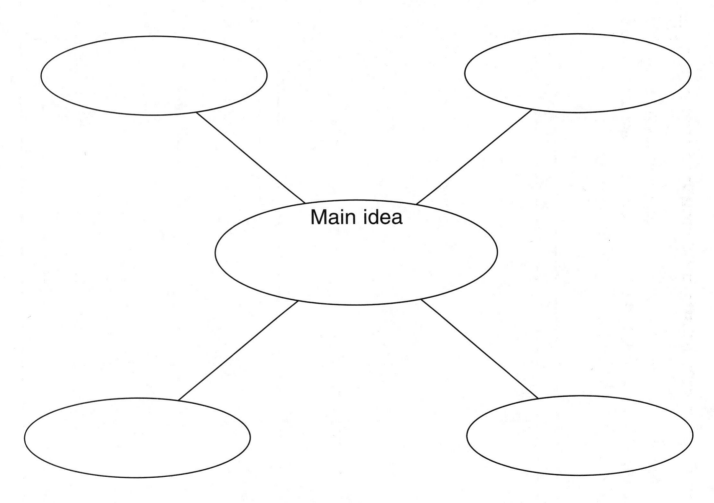

Main idea

Directions: Now use each of the small ovals above to respond to the following statements. Then draw a picture on the back of this page.

I learned a lot about _____.

I learned that _____.

I also learned that _____.

Summarize and Synthesize

Nonfiction Story Map

Directions: Make a map of the nonfiction story you just read by drawing pictures of the most important facts or events. Describe each picture in one sentence. Use your story map to paraphrase the story to a classmate.

Topic: _____

Summarize and Synthesize

Summary Cards

Directions: On each card, write one important fact or event from your book and draw a picture to go with it. Then cut the cards apart. Put the cards in order so they make sense. Last, glue the cards to another piece of paper to create a summary of the book.

Summarize and Synthesize

Compare and Summarize

Directions: In the "Topic" boxes, write the two topics you are comparing. Then, under each topic, write details that show how they are similar. Reread your information and write a one-sentence summary in the box at the bottom of the page.

Topic: _____	Topic: _____
_____	_____
_____	_____
_____	_____
_____	_____
_____	_____
_____	_____
_____	_____
_____	_____
_____	_____
_____	_____
_____	_____
_____	_____
_____	_____

Summary: _____

_____

_____

Summarize and Synthesize

Compare and Contrast

Directions: Write the two things you are comparing on the lines below. Find details from the text showing how they are alike and write them in the "Alike" column. Next find differences and write them in the "Different" column. Reread the information on the chart and write a one- to two-sentence summary in the box at the bottom of the page.

Compare _____ **and** _____

Alike	Different
_____	_____
_____	_____
_____	_____
_____	_____
_____	_____
_____	_____
_____	_____
_____	_____
_____	_____
_____	_____

Summary: _____

_____

_____

Summarize and Synthesize

Venn Diagram and Summary

Directions: Fill in the topics you are comparing over each circle. After filling in the circles with details, write a summary of what you learned.

Topic: _____   Topic: _____

Both:

Summary:

I learned a lot about _____.

I learned that _____.

I also learned that _____.

The most interesting thing I learned was _____

_____.

Summarize and Synthesize

Feature Analysis Diagram

Directions: Fill in a plus (+) or minus (–) in each box. Use the (+) to indicate that the item has the feature and use the (–) to indicate that it does not have the feature. After completing the diagram, write a summary about what you learned.

Features

Category: _____

Summary: _____

Summarize and Synthesize

Categorization Chart

Directions: Write your topic on the line below. Across the top of the chart, list some of the main ideas of the text. In the boxes below each main idea, list details that relate to each main idea.

Topic:_____

Summarize and Synthesize

Partner Reading

Directions: Write at least one sentence about what you learned. Have your partner write at least one sentence as well. Each of you should draw a picture to match your sentences.

Book title:_____

Sentence 1: _____

_____

_____

_____

Sentence 2: _____

_____

_____

_____

Picture 1:   Picture 2:

Summarize and Synthesize

Tell Me the Facts

Directions: Write one important fact in each box. This is the information you will include in your summary. Then read your summary to a partner.

Topic: _____	

Summarize and Synthesize

Summarize with the 5 Ws

Directions: Use the 5 Ws to help you determine important information about your topic.

Title or topic: _____

Who: _____

What: _____

Where: _____

When: _____

Why: _____

Use the information from the questions above to write your own short summary.

_____

_____

_____

_____

_____

_____

_____

_____

_____

_____

_____

Summarize and Synthesize

Put It in Your Own Words—Part 1

Directions: Read a nonfiction book. In your own words, tell a partner what the book was about. In three sentences, write what you think were the three most important facts you learned in this book. Make an illustration that matches your sentences.

Title: _____

1. _____

   _____

   _____

2. _____

   _____

   _____

3. _____

   _____

   _____

Summarize and Synthesize

Put It in Your Own Words—Part 2

Directions: Read each box and write the information that is asked for. Except for the title, make sure you put everything in your own words. When you are done, practice reading what you wrote so you can share it with your group.

Title:	Main idea:	One important fact:
One important fact:	One important fact:	One important fact:

Notes

PASSPORT TO COMPREHENSION

Developing Vocabulary

#50468 Successful Strategies

Developing Vocabulary

As students enter school, they bring with them vocabularies learned mainly through listening. Their speaking and listening vocabularies are usually much larger than their reading and writing vocabularies. In the primary years of school, students' vocabularies increase quickly. They are constantly being introduced to new words through reading and writing. Many of the words they encounter in their social studies, science, and other nonfiction texts will be unfamiliar to them. If students do not know the meanings of many words in expository texts, their comprehension of the content could be lost.

Vocabulary building through introduction and direct instruction helps students understand the meanings of words and succeed as readers. When new words are introduced, the teacher should use them and encourage students to use them in reading, writing, and speaking. New vocabulary must be practiced. This repetition allows students to become more familiar and comfortable with new vocabulary. They should be actively learning new words, not simply listening to the teacher read the words and their meanings.

There are numerous strategies for building vocabulary. The teacher should use a variety of these to make vocabulary building interesting and active for students. Through instruction, students will increase their vocabularies, increase comprehension, and become better readers.

Strategy 1: Picture Dictionary

Illustrations often serve as context clues for determining word meaning. As the teacher reads a text aloud for a second time, students share words they do not know. The teacher writes these words on the board. Then students go back to the text and look at the picture clues on the page where the word was used. Using these clues shows students that the words are associated with their illustrations. It is easier to understand word meanings in the context of their picture clues instead of just as a list of words. The activity on page 264 can be used to make a picture dictionary. (Standards 5.1, 5.2, 5.4, 5.6, 5.7)

Strategy 2: Word Web

A word web is a visual aid that helps students understand new information. Word webs can be used after reading to define and check understanding of new words. The new word is put into an oval in the middle of the web. It is connected to three other ovals titled: "Sentence from My Book," "Dictionary Meaning," and "Picture of My Word." A fourth oval may be added depending on the ability of the students: "My Own Sentence Using the Word." The blank word web on page 265 can be used for this strategy. (Standards 5.1, 5.4, 5.6, 5.7)

Strategy 3: Compound Word Search

As students work through a book, they can be searching for compound words. This activity could be modeled during a guided-reading lesson. The compound words can be recorded in an activity first as a whole, then as the two words that make up the compound words. All the words should be illustrated. The activity on page 266 can be used for this strategy. (Standards 5.1, 5.4, 5.6, 5.7)

Developing Vocabulary

Strategy 4: Word Detective

Use the detective sheets on pages 267 and 268. On the first Word Detective activity, have students find certain types of words, write them in the first columns, and come up with tentative definitions based upon what they know about the structure of the words. In the top-left box, the teacher must fill in the type of words he or she wants students to find as they read their books. In the second Word Detective activity, students find their vocabulary words in the dictionary and then demonstrate their understanding by using each word in a sentence. (Standards 5.4, 5.6)

Strategy 5: The Classification Game

In this activity, students work in groups. Each group is given several cards with words and pictures on them. Then they sort the cards into categories given by the teacher. For example, young students often learn about the five senses in science. They may be given the words *bitter*, *soft*, *loud*, *sweet*, *sour*, *hard*, *quiet*, and *salty*. It is important that these words are illustrated. The categories would be taste, hearing, and touch. Students would sort their cards into these categories. After the sorting is done, students need to justify why they put each card where they did. The activity on page 269 can be used for this game. The teacher writes in the categories and the words in the word bank before copying the activity, or students can fill in the categories.

In another version of the game, students are given the categories and they work together to think of words that fit each category. This game should be modeled and played together as a whole group. As students get comfortable with the game, they can play it in small groups during literacy centers. The class may have read a book on food to learn about nutrition and the food pyramid. The categories could be fruits, dairy, and bread. (Standards 5.1, 5.4, 5.6, 8.5)

Strategy 6: Word Puzzles

Students can work with their vocabulary words in puzzles. They can complete word searches and unscramble words. A word bank needs to be provided on the page with the puzzle. The Word Search template on page 270 can be used for this strategy. (Standards 5.4, 5.6, 5.7)

Strategy 7: Comic Strip

Have students write comic strips using as many of their new vocabulary words as possible. See the activity on page 271. (Standards 5.1, 5.2, 5.4, 5.6, 7.1, 7.2, 7.4)

Developing Vocabulary

Strategy 8: Using a Dictionary

Primary-grade students love to use the dictionary, but they often do not know how to use it correctly. Students should be taught that words are arranged in alphabetical order. They should also understand how to use the guide words at the top of the page to help them find a word. Once they find a word, guide them to see that there are multiple definitions for each word. This concept is difficult for young students, so teachers should choose words that they can relate to their own background knowledge. A transparency of the dictionary page can be shown on the overhead projector. Together the teacher and students find the correct definition for each word. Students can also use the dictionary independently to look up vocabulary words, record the definition, and illustrate. The activities on pages 272 and 273 are provided for practice with dictionary work. (Standards 5.4, 5.6, 7.4)

Strategy 9: Concentrate

Memory or concentration games are also fun. You can either write two sets of words onto game cards for students to match, or you can write the word on one card and the definition on the other for them to match together. There should be no more than 12 cards in a game, and students need to be taught how to set up the game in organized rows to help them to later remember where cards are for pairing. Blank game cards are provided on page 274. (Standard 5.6)

Strategy 10: Cloze Reading

Cloze sentences and passages are terrific ways to teach students how to make predictions about words that they do not know. For cloze sentences, the teacher chooses the words to be learned. Each word is written on a card with an illustration, if possible. Each card is read and students try to define the word. Definitions are written on the board and read aloud. Writing and reading the definitions help students remember the meanings. The teacher writes sentences on sentence strips using the words from the word cards. However, the words from the cards are omitted so students have to use context to try to fit each word into the correct sentence. For cloze passages, select an unfamiliar passage from a nonfiction text or textbook. Write the passage on chart paper or create an activity using the text. Leave out key words and have the class determine which word makes sense in the blank spots. This activity may be hard for students at first, and will be easier in whole-group situations where students can orally give ideas for the missing words and can listen to their classmates to get ideas. (Standards 5.2, 5.4, 5.6, 8.5)

Strategy 11: Guess the Covered Word

The teacher writes a sentence on the board with one word covered. Students guess words that would make sense in that blank. The teacher lists these guesses on the board. Next, the first letter of the covered word is revealed. Students can then eliminate words that no longer make sense in the blank. They should give reasons why the words no longer make sense. They should also suggest new words that might fit the blanks. The teacher gives hints if they do not come up with the correct word. Finally, the word is revealed. This activity can be extended to a paragraph that is taken from a text and written on chart paper. Several words can be covered up, and the activity can be repeated. (Standards 5.2, 5.4, 5.6, 5.7, 8.5)

Developing Vocabulary

Strategy 12: Picture Cards

The teacher gathers the class to sit in front of the board for a discussion. The teacher introduces the new vocabulary words, and the class discusses their meanings. Then students choose one of the new words. Students go to their seats and find the word they chose in their books. For example, in a social studies lesson in which they are learning about different words to describe bodies of water (river, ocean, lake), they find the page where the word is located. Then they draw a picture of the word on an index card. On the back of the card, they write the word and its definition. Students then work in small groups. Students take turns sharing the pictures drawn on their cards. The other students try to guess which word is illustrated. The list of possible answers is written on the board. Students record their guesses on an individual whiteboard. After everyone guesses, the student sharing his or her picture reads the word and definition from the back. The remaining students in the group share their pictures. (Standards 5.2, 5.4, 8.5)

Strategy 13: Using a Glossary

A glossary is a great resource for students to use to look up definitions. They are easier to use than a dictionary because their content is limited to the technical words used in a text. As a new unit is being introduced, the teacher finds the words that are new and important to the topic. After listing them on the board, the teacher has students turn to the glossary. As the words are found, students read the definition aloud and write it on a chart. Students can illustrate the words and put them on the chart for visual reference during the unit. Later in the school year, the teacher writes the vocabulary words and has the students work in groups to find the words. Each person in the group should be responsible for finding and defining one word, illustrating it, and sharing his or her picture so the entire group will have learned all of the words. (Standards 5.1, 5.4, 5.6, 5.7, 8.5)

Strategy 14: Word Analogies

Analogies compare relationships between words or groups of words. Teachers can introduce this concept in the primary grades by using pictures or actual items. In math, the teacher may show a ruler, a tape measure, and a thermometer and ask what they all have in common (they are used to measure). Students can suggest other items that should be in this group. The teacher may need to give clues to lead students to words that fit in the category. This process should be modeled with the teacher thinking aloud as he or she decides how the objects are related. (Standards 5.1, 5.6, 7.1, 7.4, 8.5)

Strategy 15: Select-a-Word

Select vocabulary words from an expository text that students will be reading. For example, use the vocabulary words from a chapter or lesson in their social studies book. Write the words on small strips of paper. Some words may have to be written two to three times so that you have enough for each student to have one word. Put them into a container, and have each student draw out one strip of paper. Then they write the words in their social studies response journals. Next, they read the chapter to find out what their words mean. When they think they know, they write definitions next to the words and illustrate their word. Check their work so you can help those who are having trouble using the context clues surrounding the words to figure out their meanings. Finally, have students come together as a group to present their definitions. Through sharing, the entire class is exposed to all the vocabulary words and their meanings. (Standards 5.2, 5.4, 5.6, 5.7, 8.5)

Developing Vocabulary

Strategy 16: Word Banks

Have students create their own personal word banks. You can design a word-bank system that is appropriate to your students' levels. For instance, a class of advanced writers may write words on flash cards and their meanings on the backs. A class with emerging writers can write the words on the flash cards and draw illustrations on the back. To help students form associations with the words, have them do a combination of words and pictures. For your word-bank flash cards, divide each flash card into four sections. In the top-left space, students write the vocabulary word. In the top-right space, they illustrate the word or draw a picture that represents the word. In the bottom-left space, they write the definition of the word. In the last space, they put word(s) that they personally associate with the vocabulary word. (Standards 5.1, 5.2, 5.4, 5.6, 5.7, 7.4)

mountain	⛰
highest kind of land	snow-covered, ski

Strategy 17: Multiple Meanings

Students can begin to be exposed to words with multiple meanings. Because this concept is difficult, the activities should be short and the words should be ones that students can relate to their own experiences. The following activity is good for partners and could be used at a literacy center.

Give students a list of sentences. All sentences should use the same vocabulary word, but each sentence should reflect a different meaning of the word. The partners find the word in the dictionary and then write the correct definition under each sentence. The following example uses the word *catch*: 1. I will **catch** the ball in my baseball mitt. 2. I did not **catch** the flu when my brother did. 3. The only person in our family to **catch** a fish was my sister. 4. Luckily the tree branch did not **catch** my new sweater and tear a hole in it. Students write the correct definitions of "catch" under the sentence. (Standards 5.4, 5.6, 5.7, 7.4, 8.5)

Developing Vocabulary

Picture Dictionary

Directions: Write one vocabulary word on each line. Draw a picture of each word in the space above it.

_____'s Picture Dictionary	 _____	 _____
  _____	 _____	 _____

Developing Vocabulary

Word Web

Directions: Find a new word in your book. Write it in the center oval. Fill in the web.

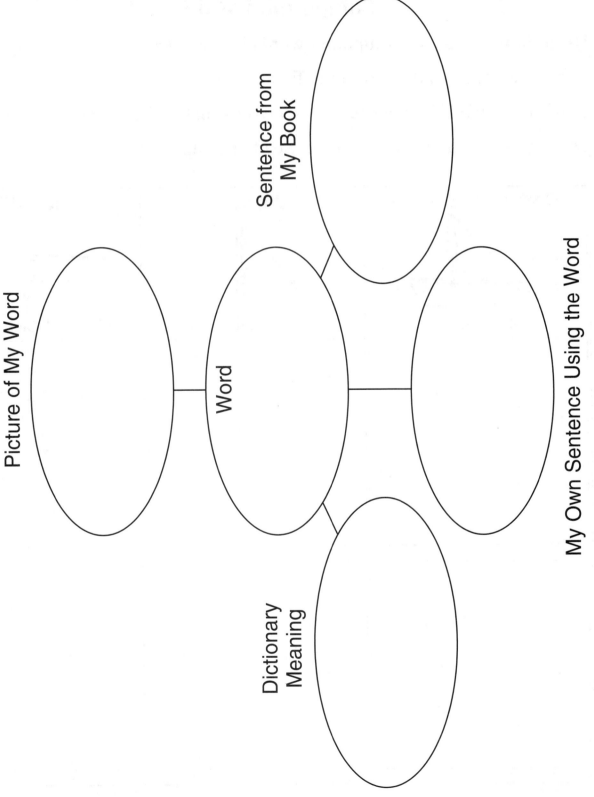

Sentence from My Book

Picture of My Word

Word

My Own Sentence Using the Word

Dictionary Meaning

Developing Vocabulary

Compound Word Search

Directions: Find two compound words in your book.

Write the compound word in the first column.

In the next two boxes, write the two words that make the compound word.

Draw a picture above each word. See the sample below.

Compound word	Word 1	Word 2
sailboat	sail	boat

Developing Vocabulary

Word Detective—Part 1

Directions: Use your book to find words that fit the heading the teacher has given you. Write what you think the word means by reading it in your book or by using what you already know about the words.

Word	Definition

Developing Vocabulary

Word Detective—Part 2

Directions: Select one of your vocabulary words and write it on the line. Find it in the dictionary. Write the page you found it on and the guide words on that page. Copy the definition exactly from the dictionary. Make up your own sentence using the word. Underline the word in the sentence.

Vocabulary word:_____

Page in dictionary:_____

Guide words: _____

Definition:_____

_____

_____

Use the word correctly in your own sentence:

_____

_____

_____

_____

Developing Vocabulary

The Classification Game

Word Bank

Developing Vocabulary

Word Search Puzzle

Directions: In the puzzle, find and circle each word from the word list.

Word List

1. _____
2. _____
3. _____

4. _____
5. _____
6. _____

Developing Vocabulary

Comic Strip

Directions: Write and illustrate a comic strip. Correctly use as many of your vocabulary words as possible when you write in the speech bubbles. The speech bubbles are drawn for you in the first box.

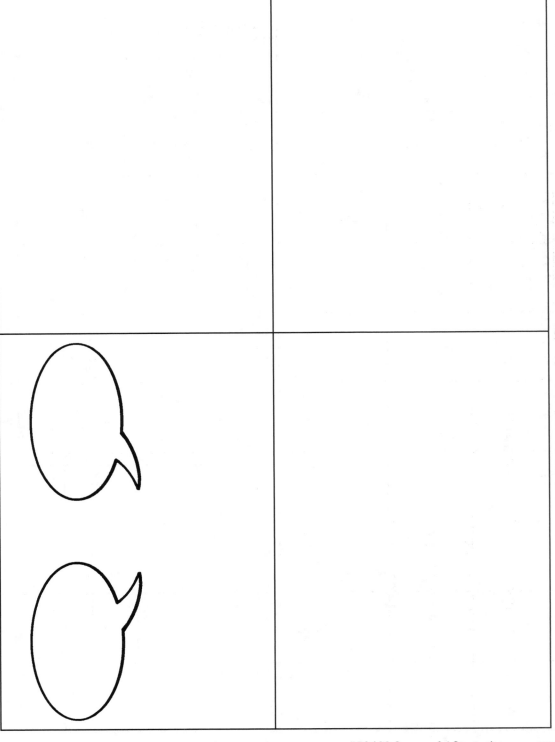

Developing Vocabulary

Using a Dictionary—Look It Up!

Directions: Pick two of your vocabulary words.

Write one on each line.

Look up each word in the dictionary.

Write the meaning of each word.

Write a sentence using the word.

Word	Meaning	Sentence
1.		
2.		

Developing Vocabulary

Using a Dictionary—I Know What That Means!

Directions:

1. Look in a book and find a word that is new to you.

2. Write what you think it means on the "My guess" line.

3. Now look up the word in the dictionary. If your guess was right, check the box. If not, write what the word means.

4. Find another word and do the same.

Word:_____	Word:_____
My guess: _____	My guess: _____
_____	_____
_____	_____
I guessed right! ❏	I guessed right! ❏
Now I know it means_____	Now I know it means_____
_____	_____
_____	_____
_____	_____
_____	_____
_____	_____

Developing Vocabulary

Concentrate

STRATEGIES
AND
SKILLS

Works Cited

Anthony, H., and T. Raphael. 1996. Using questioning strategies to promote students' active comprehension of content area material. In *Content area reading and learning: Instructional strategies*. 2nd ed. Ed, D. Lapp, J. Flood, and N. Farnan, 307–22. Upper Saddle River, NJ: Allyn and Bacon.

Baker, L. 2002. Metacognition in comprehension instruction. In *Comprehension instruction: Research-based best practices*, ed. C. C. Block and M. Pressley, 77–95. New York: Guilford Press.

Baker, L., and A. L. Brown. 1984. Metacognitive skills and reading. In *Handbook of reading research*, ed. P. D. Pearson, R. Barr, M. L. Kamil, and P. Mosenthal, 353–94. Mahwah, NJ: Lawrence Erlbaum.

Block, C. C. 1999. Comprehension: Crafting understanding. In *Best practices in literacy instruction*, ed. L. B. Gambrell, L. M. Morrow, S. B. Neuman, and M. Pressley, 98–118. New York: Guilford Press.

Cunningham, P., and R. Allington. 1999. Classrooms that work: They can all read and write. 2nd ed. Boston: Addison-Wesley Educational Publishers, Inc.

Dole, J. A., K. J. Brown, and W. Trathen. 1996. The effects of strategy instruction on the comprehension performance of at-risk students. *Reading Research Quarterly* 31 (1): 62–88.

Duke, N. K., and P. D. Pearson. 2002. Effective practices for developing reading comprehension. In *What research has to say about reading instruction*. 3rd ed. Ed. A. E. Farstup and S. J. Samuels, 205–42. Newark, DE: International Reading Association, Inc.

Durkin, D. 1978. What classroom observations reveal about reading comprehension instruction. *Reading Research Quarterly* 14 (4): 481–533.

Fountas, I., and G. Pinnell. 2001. *Guiding readers and writers grades 3–6*. Portsmouth, NH: Heinemann.

Garner, R. 1987. *Metacognition and reading comprehension*. Norwood, NJ: Ablex.

Harvey, S. 1998. *Nonfiction matters*. Portland, ME: Stenhouse.

Harvey, S., and A. Goudvis. 2000. *Strategies that work*. Portland, ME: Stenhouse.

Holmes, B. C., and N. L. Roser. 1987. Five ways to assess readers' prior knowledge. *The Reading Teacher* 40 (7): 646–49.

Keene, E. O. 2002. From good to memorable: Characteristics of highly effective comprehension teaching. In *Improving comprehension instruction*, ed. C. C. Block, L. B. Gambrell, and M. Pressley, 80–105. San Francisco: Jossey-Bass.

Keene, E., and S. Zimmerman. 1997. *Mosaic of thought*. Portsmouth, NH: Heinemann

Kragler, S., C. A. Walker, and L. E. Martin. 2005. Strategy instruction in primary content textbooks. *The Reading Teacher* 59 (3): 254–61.

Works Cited

Mastropieri, M. A., and T. E. Scruggs. 1997. Best practices in promoting reading comprehension in students with learning disabilities. *Remedial and Special Education* 18 (4): 197–214.

McCarthy, S., L. Hoffman, and J. Galda. 1999. Readers in elementary classrooms: Learning goals and instructional principles. In *Engaged reading*, ed. J. Guthrie and D. Alvermann, 46–80. New York: Teachers College Press.

National Reading Panel. 2000. *Teaching children to read: An evidence-based assessment of the scientific research literature on reading and its implications for reading instruction—reports of the subgroups.* Washington, DC: National Institute of Child Health and Human Development.

Naughton, V. 1993. Creative mapping for content reading. *Journal of Reading* 37 (4): 324–26.

Paris, S. G., B. A. Wasik, and J. C. Turner. 1991. The development of strategic readers. In vol. 2 of *Handbook of reading research,* ed. R. Barr, M. L. Kamil, P. Mosenthal, and P. D. Pearson, 609–40. Mahwah, NJ: Lawrence Erlbaum.

Pearson, P. D., and D. D. Johnson. 1978. *Teaching reading comprehension.* New York: Holt, Reinhart, and Winston.

Pressley, M. 2000. What should comprehension instruction be the instruction of? In vol. 3 of *Handbook of reading research,* ed. R. Barr, M. L. Kamil, P. B. Mosenthal, and P. D. Pearson, 545–62. Mahwah, NJ: Lawrence Erlbaum.

———. 2002. Metacognition and self-regulated comprehension. In *What reasearch has to say about reading instruction.* 3rd ed. Ed. A. E. Farstrup and S. J. Samuels, 291–309. Newark, DE: International Reading Association, Inc.

Pressley, M., and P. Afflerbach. 1995. *Verbal protocols for reading: The nature of constructively responsive reading.* Hillsdale, NJ: Lawrence Erlbaum.

Rasinksi, T., and N. Padak. 2000. *Effective reading strategies: Teaching children who find reading difficult.* 2nd ed. Columbus, OH: Merrill/Prentice Hall.

Readence, J. E., T. W. Bean, and R. S. Baldwin. 1998. *Content area literacy: An integrated approach.* 6th ed. Dubuque, IA: Kendall/Hunt Publishing.

Robb, L. 2000. *Teaching reading in the middle school: A strategic approach to teaching reading that improves comprehension and thinking.* New York: Scholastic Professional Books.

Rose, L. 1991. *Picture this for beginning readers: Teaching reading through visualization.* Brookline, MA: Zephyr Press.

Schraw, G. 1998. Promoting general metacognitive awareness. *Instructional Science* 26 (1–2): 113–25

Schwartz, R. M., and T. Raphael. 1985. Concept of definition: A key to improving students' vocabulary. *The Reading Teacher* 39 (2): 198–205.

Tarasoff, M. 1993. *Reading instruction that makes sense.* Active Learning Institute.